GUIDING KINDERGARTEN CHILDREN IN THE CHURCH SCHOOL

A COOPERATIVE TEXT

Guiding
Kindergarten Children

IN THE

Church School

by Elizabeth McE. Shields

Revised by Dorothae G. Mallard

Published for the Cooperative Publication Association

by

JOHN KNOX PRESS
RICHMOND, VIRGINIA

This is one of a series of books produced for interdenominational use by the Protestant denominations working through the Cooperative Publication Association.

Library of Congress Catalog Card Number: 54-10894

First printing, 1931

Second printing, 1932

Third printing, 1935

Fourth printing, 1940

Fifth printing, 1947

Sixth printing, 1949

Seventh printing, 1952

Eighth printing, revised edition, 1955

Ninth printing, 1955

Tenth printing, 1957

Eleventh printing, 1958

Printed in the United States of America

5885-(20)-D.309

Contents

Chapter I

Our Purpose in Teaching Little Children

Chapter II

How Children Learn

Chapter III

A Group of Kindergarten Children

Chapter IV

The Leaders of a Kindergarten Group

Chapter V

The Children's Room for Work and Play and Worship

Chapter VI

Conversation: An Experience Which Aids the
Religious Growth of Children

Chapter VII

Worship: An Experience Which Aids the
Religious Growth of Children

Chapter VIII

Listening to Stories: An Experience Which Aids the Religious Growth of Children

Chapter IX

Using Music: An Experience Which Aids the Religious Growth of Children

Chapter X

Other Experiences Which Aid the Religious Growth of Children

Chapter XI

Planning and Carrying Out Informal Procedure

Chapter XII

Parents and Teachers Working Together

CHAPTER I

Our Purpose in Teaching Little Children

REACH DOWN YOUR HAND

Reach down your hand!
The little one who trudges by your side
Is striving hard to match your grown-up stride;
But, oh, his feet are very tiny yet,
His arm so short—I pray you, don't forget—
Reach down your hand!

Keep soft your voice!
For it was such a little while ago
This small one left the place where tones are low;
His voice still holds the cadence of that land
Where no one ever gave a stern command—
Keep soft your voice!

Lift up your heart!
The little child you struggle so to teach
Has resource far above the human reach;
Lift up your heart!

—*Lucie Haskell Hill.*[1]

A Specific Purpose

Picture Number One

There was the sound of chimes in the church tower; the sunshine poured through the clear glass of the east windows; the Kindergarten superintendent stood waiting in the room that was the children's very own in the church school—their very own even when the children were not present, for its

---

[1] From *Children* (now *Parents' Magazine*). Used by permission.

atmosphere silently spoke of them. Soon, however, the children began to come, singly, in pairs and in groups. As they arrived, they went over to a small table at the front of the room where some flowers, a basket, and a Bible were attractively placed. They dropped their money into the basket and most of them were immediately attracted to some bright pictures on the picture rail.

"Oh, they are birdies!" exclaimed a happy little voice, and soon a number of children were touching the pictures, asking questions of Miss Jean and her helpers and giving information about the birds they happened to know.

By and by a child discovered the picture of a bird's nest, and his discovery brought from quiet Arthur a piece of information that electrified the children, the teacher, and the helpers:

"I saw one this morning, out in that tree!"

Quickly Miss Jean eliminated from her morning program the last year's bird's nest carefully reposing in the cupboard, waiting to be introduced at the proper time, and calling the children to her, she said, "Arthur has found a bird's nest in the yard and wants to show it to us. Let's go with him." So teacher, children, and helpers went into the yard and stood under the tree where they could examine the nest. The children decided that it was made of sticks, leaves, grass, and one bit of paper.

"Let's gather sticks, leaves, and grass, and a piece of paper for a nest," was the adult suggestion, eagerly received by the children.

It took some time to find just the kind of sticks and grass a bird would use, but soon with the help of each there was a reasonable supply, which was placed on the ground in the center of the group.

"Can you make a bird's nest?" was the teacher's question.

There was an uncertain touching of the sticks and grass and a look of uncertainty on the faces of the children until Bobby eagerly said, "I think *I* can make one."

"All right, Bobby, you may try," was the answer.

"But I'll have to have a bush or something to put it in," said the little fellow.

A bush was found nearby, but, as Bobby was about to begin, a doubt of his ability seemed to cross his mind and he said, "I don't believe I *really* can," and sat down again.

Several of the other children began trying to put the grass and sticks together. Arthur went so far as to lift his and try to put it in the bush, but it fell to pieces. There was much disappointment in his voice as he said, "I can't do it." And the others agreed with him.

The teacher waited patiently while they came to this decision, and then she turned to one of her assistants and asked, "Can *you* build a nest?" The answer came back, "I am sure I cannot." Then, while a hush was on the group, she said, "*We* don't know how to build nests that birds will use. God planned it so that birds would know how to build their nests. He has planned for people to do things that birds cannot do and birds to do things that people cannot do. It is very wonderful."

Then she told the following story:

The birds went, "Chee, chee, chee, chee," and Jimmy was listening.

They were in the apple tree at the side of the house—a mother bird and a father bird.

The mother bird flew down to the ground and picked up a piece of grass and flew back into the tree. Then very quickly the father bird followed her and caught up a little stick or twig in his bill—and Jimmy was watching.

"What are the birds doing, Mother?" asked Jimmy.

"They are building a nest," Mother said.

"What is a nest, Mother?"

"A nest is a home for baby birds. After a while the birds will finish their home and you can see it if you are careful not to touch it."

The birds flew back and forth to different places in the yard. They put each stick and bit of grass and piece of string into place until a beautiful nest was made, and all the time Jimmy was watching.

"Who showed them how to do that?" he asked, and his eyes were bright.

"It was God. He made the birds in such a way that they know how to build their bird homes or nests. It's wonderful, isn't it, Jimmy?"

Jimmy's eyes had a look that eyes have when a person is thinking about God, and he said softly, "Yes, it is wonderful!"

He had the same look in his eyes one day when Mother let him climb with her on the stepladder to peep carefully into the birds' home when mother and father bird were away. They saw three blue eggs.

"It's wonderful, isn't it, Jimmy?" Mother said again, and Jimmy said softly, "Yes, it is wonderful."

He had the same look in his eyes when the baby birds came out of the eggs and the mother and father bird sang their very sweetest songs. He felt like singing, too.

He did sing, too. He and Mother sang:

> "All things bright and beautiful,
> All things large and small,
> All things wise and wonderful,
> Our God has planned them all." [2]

While the story was being told, the teacher could tell by the looks on the faces of the children that she was sharing some worth-while knowledge and was enriching the experiences through which the group was living. At the end of the story, very quietly Miss Jean said, "I would like to talk to God about it," and there was a feeling of worship as she voiced a simple prayer of wonder and gratitude to God for His care of birds. When they came back into the room it seemed most natural that they should gather about the piano while the pianist played "All Things Bright and Beautiful." There was real appreciation of the song as they sang it.

The teacher glanced at the clock and saw it was almost time for dismissal. Before they left, the children looked at pictures of birds found on the table. At Miss Jean's suggestion they tried to pick out in the pictures things bright and beautiful and large and small. After singing the song again, they left for home, many of them happily singing the song as they went.

The teacher and her helpers remained a few minutes to put the pictures in order and to answer the questions of a visiting friend who had been present throughout the hour.

"It seemed almost as if it all just happened, and yet you must have had some plan. Did you have a plan, or did it just

---

[2] C. F. Alexander. Found in most songbooks for children. Last line adapted.

happen that pictures, conversation, story, and music all seemed to help to do one thing?"

"Yes, I had a plan, but my purpose was bigger and more important than my plan. I think Arthur helped to carry out my purpose better than I could have carried it out unaided by him."

"I see what you mean. Even though the children would never connect it with a 'purpose,' I believe the youngest child in the group went home feeling, 'Isn't it wonderful that God has planned it so that birds know how to build nests?' Perhaps a few of them even put it into words. What would your plan have been if Arthur had not discovered the nest in such a timely way?"

Miss Jean went to the cabinet and took out her treasured last year's nest, and said, "This would have helped. I would have used it in place of the new one."

"I believe," said the visitor, "that if I had been prepared with a last year's nest, I should not have had the judgment to change to Arthur's discovery. I should probably have acknowledged his statement courteously and then proceeded to show *my* discovery."

Miss Jean laughed and said, "You are doing yourself an injustice, I am sure, but I must admit that it took me a long time to make a distinction between plans and purposes—to hold my plan in abeyance while I adhered to my purpose and to watch for the leading of the children in carrying out my purpose."

There was more talk about where to find suitable story material, songs, pictures, and so forth; and then the friends parted.

Picture Number Two

Miss Brown, the Kindergarten superintendent, rushed into the Kindergarten room breathless, to find many of the children already there. There was nothing about the room to specially mark it as a happy meeting place for children. A few framed pictures, mostly copies of old masterpieces, were hung high on the walls. The chairs were all stiffly set in a circle and some of them were occupied by listless children. Other children were aimlessly wandering around the room and two were engaged in a tussling match. Although the lesson was about "God's Care of Birds," there were no pictures or anything else to stimulate interest in birds.

Miss Brown called the children to the circle of chairs as one of her helpers, the pianist, walked in. They started their usual Sunday morning routine, singing "Good Morning" and "Praise Him" and then having a prayer in which each child was supposed to thank God for something. Next followed the song, "Jesus Loves Me," and the offering, when the children marched around and put their money into the basket which Miss Brown held. There was delay and confusion as they searched their pockets for their money, some dropping it and scrambling to retrieve it and some loudly insisting they had money but couldn't find it.

After they had sung the song, "Love Gifts," Miss Brown said, "Everybody sit down and I'll read you a story. Our lesson today is 'God's Care of Birds.'" Immediately Peter spoke up, "Oh, Miss Brown, there are two birds in our back yard!" The teacher frowned, "You must not interrupt me, Peter; it isn't polite," and then she proceeded to read the story from her teacher's guide.

At the end of the story she said, "Now, if you will learn your memory work well today, maybe we'll have time to color some birds." Then she started drilling the children on saying the Twenty-third Psalm. After about ten minutes of this, during which the children became quite restless and noisy, she took them to the tables to color the birds which she had traced. She gave many admonitions about staying exactly within the lines and about the right colors to use. When Peter made his bird brown with an orange breast because that was the kind of bird he had seen in his back yard, she gave him another, saying, "Color it blue like I told you."

By that time the bell rang for dismissal and the children jumped up and ran for the door, many of them forgetting to take their birds, and many rushing right past the helper who was trying to give out some leaflets as the children went out.

Miss Brown sank down in a chair and said to her helper, "I declare it seems like it gets harder every Sunday to keep the children quiet and make them listen to the lesson." To her the lesson was the story. Although the title of the lesson was "God's Care of Birds," the only connection she made with that thought was the story and the coloring of the birds. It never occurred to her that everything in the session could contribute to the definite purpose of helping the children feel the wonder and appreciation of God's plan for birds. If you had asked her, "Did you have a plan for today?" she would have been surprised that you did not know, for she has a plan for every Sunday and it is the same plan—exactly the same routine every week. The only variation is a change in the story and the addition once in a while of some handwork. Had you asked her, "What was your purpose for today?" she would have been at a loss for a proper reply. After thought, her answer might have been, "To help the children worship God and to teach the Bible."

Admitting that this was her purpose, her plan in carrying it out was certainly a very poor one. And if the stated purpose for the day was really her purpose, it was much too general to be accomplished in one week.

Let us compare this vague, general purpose with the specific, definite purpose of "Miss Jean," stated by her visitor as she voiced the thoughts of the children, "Isn't it wonderful that God has planned it so that birds know how to build nests?" Can you not visualize the difference in development of the two groups in their two years' experience in the Kindergarten of the church school? The children under the leadership of Miss Jean are not being introduced to generalities: they are being helped day by day to meet specific problems. They are living through rich experiences.

Specific Purposes Lead to General Goals

For each session the teacher should have a definite purpose in mind—something she hopes will be accomplished in the thoughts, feelings, and actions of her children; and all the activities she uses in that session should help to accomplish that purpose. Obviously these session purposes cannot cover too much ground or be too general, because little children must be led step by step toward the goals of religious education.

So there are long-term goals toward which the Kindergarten teacher should strive as she guides the children and shares experiences with them during the two years they spend with her. The purpose of each session will help build toward one or more of these goals, so that by the end of the two years the children will have been guided along all the ways toward a knowledge and love of God, Jesus, the Bible, the church, and a more Christlike way of living in their everyday experiences.

Goals for the Christian Education of Kindergarten Children

1. What do we want our children to think and feel about God?

We want to help our children to begin to think of God as one who is wise and loving, and who made them and all people and creatures in the world; who planned the world with all its wonder and beauty to be a home for people— working through people to provide food, clothing, shelter and warmth, and all other needs, and providing for the needs of all His creatures; who lets children and older people help Him in caring for His world by helping themselves and others; who is good and expects them to be good; who wants children to talk with Him any time and anywhere about things that make them happy or unhappy, or about things that are hard to do; who is ready and anxious to forgive them when they are sorry for wrong things they have done.

2. What do we want our children to think and feel about Jesus?

We want to help our children to think of Jesus, God's Son, as the best friend of little children; who was once a little baby; who grew as other boys grow; who became a man and went about doing good; who came to help us know God better; who lets children help Him today by doing kind and thoughtful things for others. We want them to love Jesus and desire to grow like Him in work and play.

3. What do we want our children to think and feel about the Bible?

We want to help our children to think of the Bible as the special book that contains stories about God and Jesus and about people who have learned to know God and live in right ways; as the book which is different from other books because it tells about God and His world and what is right and what is wrong. We want them to grow in their desire to learn more of what is in the Bible; and to act in right ways because of the teaching of the stories and verses which God has given in His Bible.

4. What do we want our children to think and feel about the church?

We want to help our children to have happy experiences at the church school; to develop an appreciation and love for the church; to begin to think of it as a group of people who love God and Jesus and who try to do what God wants them to do; to enjoy coming to the church to learn and talk and sing about God; to feel themselves a part of the church, and to develop a sense of responsibility for their conduct and work in their group at church.

5. How do we want our children to develop in their own personal Christian growth?

We want to help our children to try to lead more Christlike lives; to develop a sense of right and wrong and a desire to do right; to realize that God is interested in their conduct and will help them think of right ways to act and will forgive them if they are sorry when they do wrong; to recognize themselves as a part of God's plan and grow in their ability to help themselves and others.

6. How do we want our children to feel and act toward other people and groups?

We want our children to realize that it is God's plan that people should live happily with others, sharing with and helping each other; to think of their families as their friends to whom they will show love and kindness; to appreciate the help of their families and of other workers who contribute to their welfare; to grow in their awareness of the rights of others; to learn that God created and loves all people of the world and He wants them to love and help other people, regardless of their color or race.

For Assignment and Discussion

1. If possible visit a Kindergarten in a church school, or if you are now teaching Kindergarten in the church school, go over last Sunday's session, and note (1) the purpose which was evident throughout the session; (2) the materials and activities used to achieve that purpose; (3) the responses and actions of the children which showed any desired outcomes.

2. Examine the teacher's quarterly or manual for the present quarter and check the situations or "lessons" given there against the goals listed in this chapter, with a view to discovering which of these goals we might reasonably hope to achieve through the use of this material and the methods suggested for its use.

Helpful Books

The Opening Doors of Childhood, Sherrill
Understanding Children, Sherrill
The Faith of Our Children, Jones
Our Little Child Faces Life, Odell
Your Child Grows Toward God, Rosser
Tell Me About God, Jones
Tell Me About Jesus, Jones
Tell Me About the Bible, Jones
The Children We Teach, Whitehouse
Goals for the Religious Education of Children, National Council of Churches of Christ

CHAPTER II

How Children Learn

There are laws which govern the growth and development of children—physical, mental, and spiritual. No human being has made these laws. They are as unchangeable as the law of gravitation or the laws governing the germination of seed and the growth of plants. They are made by God and thoughtful people have discovered them. The teacher needs to think about these laws as she considers how her children learn.

Ways of Learning

Doing

Children learn best through experience, through doing things for themselves. The child who has a chance to try out something learns that thing much faster and better than one who is just told about it. How could a child ever learn to read and write without actually having the experience of trying to read and write? This is true of older people, too. One could hardly become a good driver of a car just by reading the manual—he must have the experience of actually sitting behind the wheel and driving many times before he has really learned to be a good driver.

This is just as true when children are learning Christian virtues. They may say the words, "Be kind to one another,"[1] over and over, but until they have many experiences of being kind to others and having others be kind to them, they may do like the little boy who was shouting the Bible verse, "Be

[1] Ephesians 4:32, R.S.V. This and other quotations from the Revised Standard Version are copyrighted by the Division of Christian Education of the National Council of the Churches of Christ in the United States of America.

kind to one another," at the top of his voice and at the same time was pinching the child next to him.

Using the Senses

Young children learn through their senses. They see and hear and feel and smell and taste. Although it is part of God's wonderful plan that they should learn in all of these ways, adults often take the attitude that children may look and listen, but they must not touch or feel. How is a child to learn roughness or smoothness, hardness or softness, the varying degrees of size and shape, without using his hands to feel? Any teacher who has tried to show a picture to Kindergarten children knows how several will always jump up, saying, "Let me hold it" or "Let me touch it."

One Sunday a child brought a huge yellow chrysanthemum to church school. Very carefully she put the flower in a vase and placed it on the beauty center table in the front of the room. Many of the children admired the lovely flower. One small boy saw the chrysanthemum as he was about to place his money in the offering basket on the table. He stood for a moment just looking at it, then he dropped his money on the table instead of into the basket and cupped both his hands around the flower, moving them gently to feel its softness. He leaned over to bury his nose in its fragrance, then, glancing around to see if anyone was looking, he stuck out his tongue and let it glide over the petals. This seemed to satisfy him, and taking a deep breath he turned around and started over to the block corner. He had learned much about that flower through his senses.

Observing and Imitating

Children learn many things as they observe adults and other children around them. As they observe, they imitate.

Lucy learns to hold her fork as Mother does, and learns to speak in Aunt Lucy's whining tone of voice.

Ned learns to bow his head when Miss B. talks to God from seeing what the others do.

A little boy learns to swear from a workman on his street.

A little girl learns to dislike her pastor from conversation of adults at the dinner table.

A child learns to speak softly from listening to his mother and father.

A little boy learns to quarrel from two playmates next door.

A child learns to lift the baby carefully by watching his older sister.

A little girl learns to fear storms by living with a fearful aunt.

Children learn also from observation of their surroundings. "It is all right to scatter paper over the church school floor—it always has scraps of paper on it." "These books already have some crayon marks in them—so it will be all right to mark them up some more." The order or lack of order, the beauty or lack of beauty of the homes and church schools in which little children are placed are powerful teachers, even though those who are responsible may not be conscious of the fact.

Suggestion and Precept

Children learn through suggestion.

One Sunday morning the children were overstimulated and became too noisy. They decided to play church, and the leader was much concerned lest the "church service" should suffer from thoughtlessness. So she said, suiting the action to the words,

> "Very softly I will walk,
> Very gently I will talk,
> When to church I go." [2]

Then she said, "Mary, show me how you walk when you go to church," and, as was to be expected, Mary walked very softly, as did the other children when they took their places in the play church.

It was clean-up time in the Kindergarten but many of the children who had been playing with the blocks did not seem interested in putting them away. The teacher started to pick up a few blocks, singing to the tune of "London Bridge"—

> Clean-up time and I will help,
> I will help, I will help.
> Clean-up time and I will help;
> Who else will help?

[2] Used by permission of the American Baptist Publication Society.

and several children immediately started picking up the blocks.

There are many precepts which we hope our boys and girls will learn, such as "Be kind" and "Love one another." But it is much better to teach these through the power of suggestion than by drilling on the words. Mentioning often to the children, "Be kind," as they go about their work and play will reap rewards in desired conduct, which is the goal for which we are striving rather than the mere repetition of words.

Suggestions which cannot be named, much less classified, come to children on every hand. It is easy for them to learn through suggestion because it is an indirect method. It leaves to the learner the power to make his own choices—a prerogative which is clung to tenaciously, even in the early years.

For example, John hears a story of "Ben," a boy of his own age who puts away his toys, wipes the mud from his shoes, and, in many ways, exhibits a spirit of helpfulness. No moral is tacked on, but John thinks to himself, "I'm going to be like Ben." Thus through the power of suggestion he learns to admire helpfulness, and through his natural tendency to imitate he begins to practice this virtue, and a happy mother reports to the church school teacher, "I don't know what has done it, but John is learning to be helpful."

Assimilating Information

Children also learn from direct information given to them by the teacher or other people. Years ago many teachers felt this was the only way to teach and spent the whole time talking to the children. Today there are some who, in their enthusiasm for using indirect methods, go to the other extreme and do not give enough information which only a thoughtful adult can supply.

A child will learn through information he uses rather than that which he just hears. Also he is more apt to use it and thus assimilate it if he has some reason to desire the particular information given. As a rule, he shows this desire or readiness through questions. On the other hand, a little child may fire so many questions, one after another, that he does not have time to assimilate the information he receives.

Perhaps one of the most difficult problems in teaching is to decide "when" and "how much" and "how" to give information. Usually if it is given in response to a question or some other indication of readiness and in terms the child can understand, he will assimilate it and make it a part of himself.

It is true that, oftentimes, a mental and spiritual "readiness" may have to be brought about so that the information can be received by the child as a part of his experience. For example, the information, "God cares for His children at all times—in the happy daytime and in the quiet nighttime," will not be accepted by the child unless it is made a part of his experience; so we help him to build up a background or readiness for this information. Perhaps we look at pictures of the nighttime, possibly of a little child asleep; we play that it is the happy daytime; in imagination the dark has come, and we are going to sleep; a lullaby of God's care is sung; after a few minutes we wake and listen to a story of God's care at night, and sing "God, Our Father, Cares." We then talk about some of the ways God cares for His children at night—through the family who helps take care of them and through people who work at night. After this the information, "God cares for His children at all times—in the happy daytime and in the quiet nighttime," is really assimilated. It is then a part of the children's imaginary experience, which is, of course, very close to a little child's real life—so close that in many cases the information is taken over into his everyday or every-night experience.

Reasoning

Nancy Elizabeth was five years old. Her Christmas doll had not only filled her heart with delight but had started an interesting train of thought.

"If I am Dollie's mother, what are you?" she asked her mother.

"I must be her grandmother," was the answer of the mother with imagination.

"And Daddy is the grandfather," the little five-year-old continued. "Who is Frederick?" (Her older brother.)

"He must be her uncle," the mother patiently co-operated.

When the older sister was classified as Dollie's aunt, a thoughtful look came into Nancy Elizabeth's eyes and she said, "Well, Santa Claus must be Dollie's 'God' for he made her."

A little child is not always credited with the power to reason, and yet very early in life he begins to act on a reasoning basis. He cries. Mother takes him up; and so the next time he wants to be taken up he cries again. Five years later he goes to the table without washing his face and reasons that he may escape the usual penalty of going back to the bathroom—because once Mother did not send him.

Many of the mistakes which children make are caused by learning through reasoning when they have not sufficient data on which to base their reasoning, or because they are not yet experienced enough to assimilate certain facts that have been presented to them or to which they have been "exposed." All reasoning is linked with observation. The child who learned that "David doesn't quarrel when he plays" made the connection between the two. He had played with David several times happily. He observed at those times that David did not try to grab his toys or quarrel, and so, reason stepped in and deduced that "David doesn't quarrel when he plays."

Some grownups expect little children to be reasonable beings from an adult standpoint, and are disappointed when they do not find them so. Some adults, on the other hand, are wise enough to build on the child's ability to reason in a limited way. It is only when we realize the possibilities, as well as the limitations, of a little child's reasoning that we can make the most of this ability in his religious education. Perhaps one day a mother will talk to her child of the kindest person they know, and say, "He tries to do the things God wants him to do." Another day she will introduce him to the most helpful person she knows and say, "She tries to do the things God wants her to do." Again she will show him the things God has created and talk to him of His care. All the time the child's reason is functioning, and by and by he reasons, "God is good." This is not because she made him say so, but because she helped him to think so. He has learned through reasoning.

Steps to Learning

There are definite steps or laws which are used in situations in which learning takes place.

Readiness

First there is the step of readiness. What is it that causes Lanny to learn to ride a tricycle?

Observation of other children has something to do with his desire to learn, but on the other hand he has not the same desire to do everything he sees done, and so "observation" is not alone responsible. There is something in him—something that drives him irresistibly to attempt the fascinating experience of putting his hands on the bars and working his feet up and down. He is eager to see if he can "make it go, too." He wants to learn to ride a tricycle and so, without doubt, he can and will learn.

Wanting to learn is the biggest essential in the learning process. No amount of desire to teach on the part of the teacher will make up for a keen desire to learn on the part of the learner. There must be a drive from within—a something that we call "readiness"—before learning can take place. The child must be interested in the thing to be learned or the teacher's efforts will be to no avail.

Of course there are many ways of bringing about readiness. Often objects or pictures can be provided to arouse curiosity and interest. Many incentives can be used. But a teacher needs to distinguish between good and bad incentives to motivate learning. For example, there are several possible incentives or ways of causing a child to want to say the Bible verse, "God is my helper." The first, and absolutely wrong, incentive is that of competition, and yet it is quite easy to cause a child to want to repeat the verse because another child has done so. Egoism may also cause him to want to repeat the verse because "Miss Margaret [a visitor] should like to see how well you can say it," but this also is not a high incentive. Cannot a way be discovered of helping him to want to know the verse because of what the verse will mean to him in his daily life? Perhaps the verse can be linked with a situation which can be pictured for him in words— a situation in which some other child used it naturally.

For example, the following illustration might be used:

Peter was lost. He had run after a little dog, hoping to catch him, and he hadn't looked where he was going. Now he couldn't see where the dog had gone and as he looked around he didn't know where he was. His eyes filled with tears and he sat down on the curb to cry. But all of a sudden he thought of a Bible verse he had learned, "God is my helper." He asked God to help him now. He thought a minute, and said to himself, "Crying won't help. I'll have to think of something to do." Just then he saw a policeman in the next block. He jumped up and ran to the policeman. He told him his name and where he lived, and in just a little while he was back safe at home. When he talked with Mother about it, she said, "I'm glad you thought about God being your helper. That is one way He helps—by helping you think of what to do."

Then the teacher can say, "There are many times when I, too, love to think 'God is my helper'; I say it over and over again, 'God is my helper.' Perhaps you will want to say the words softly with me, so that many times this week you can say them to yourself." Thus there may be a "readiness," not only to say the words, but to accept the comfort conveyed in the words.

In most learning experiences the incentive to learn is not fostered by an adult who is consciously teaching. The natural curiosity of a child leads him into avenues of investigation and achievement through which he learns daily. It is for us to follow him in his learning, and to discover and use the "readiness" which is already driving him forward.

Effect

The second step is summed up in the law of effect. Very early in life, as the child goes about doing things he begins to understand that some of his undertakings are failures and some are successes. He does not of course think of the words "success" or "failure," but he thinks whatever corresponds to them in a little child's terminology. Perhaps he thinks "fun," "good time," "I like it," for success; and "no fun," or "hurts," or "I don't like it," for failure. At any rate, he is classifying his experiences, and those that are "nice" and that he "likes" are the ones he will be glad to repeat, while those that are "no fun" or that he does not "like" or that have something unpleasant associated with them will not be repeated by him, if he has the choice. So the teacher must try to see to it that the child gains satisfaction from his learning experiences in the church school.

Activity

The third step in the learning process is following the law of activity. A child must do for himself if he is to really learn. At the beginning of this chapter, experience or doing was listed as one of the most important ways of learning. The old adage, "Experience is the best teacher," still holds true. A child learns best when he is self-active in the learning process.

Practice

The last step is practice or repetition. "Practice makes perfect." The child, Lanny, who was learning to ride the tricycle, would have to do it many times before he acquired enough skill to say, "I can really ride a tricycle."

When the church school teacher wishes her children to learn to be helpful, she will have to provide many experiences in which they can actually practice helpfulness before she can feel that they are learning this Christian trait.

Learning Many Things at One Time

Educational procedure would not be so complicated were it not for the fact that a child learns many things at one time. On the other hand, because this is true, it is much more interesting to watch the all-round character development that comes as a result.

An illustration of learning many things at once is found in

a project carried on by a Kindergarten group in a vacation church school. They decided to make a gift for their pastor. The teacher thought of it primarily as a project in building up a happy relationship between the group and the minister. The children were very happy in learning to share with their minister, but they were also learning many other things. Their immediate attention was focused on making a cushion. They learned how to cut irregular pieces of oilcloth for the flowers and how to tear paper in small bits to serve as "stuffing."

Probably if any child had been asked as he reached home, "What did you learn today?" the answer would have been, "I learned to tear paper and cut flowers for a cushion." In many cases the parent who received this answer might think, "And they call that teaching religion!" Perhaps this same parent might have felt quite differently if he had received the teacher's answer to "What did your children learn today?" This teacher would have said, "They learned to think more of their minister. They are beginning to learn the valuable lesson of co-operation. They could not all have the scissors at one time, nor could they all do the same things, and so they found that by putting all their efforts together the result was something beautiful. They would not know the word 'co-operation' if they heard it, but nevertheless they are learning to co-operate."

Co-operation, of course, is most valuable, but it was not the attitude the leader set out to develop. It came about as part of the project. It was a necessary part of the lessons which the making of the cushion taught—affection for their pastor, a desire to share with him, and loyalty to their church.

The Teacher's Part and God's Part

It is significant that in the very wording of the heading of this chapter the emphasis has been put upon the learner.

The teacher, it is true, is important—important because, if she is a true teacher, she stands ready to share a wealth of experience, to guide the children into situations in which they will grow in knowledge and experience, situations where they may repeatedly live the things they are learning until they habitually do right because it is pleasing to God.[3]

In the learning of spiritual things, the work of God's Spirit should not be minimized. Without His help the spiritual could never be taught. He is the Teacher. He does, however, often work through other people and in the circumstances that surround His children. Those who are teachers may be co-workers with Him. What a happy, fascinating work it is to which they are called—to stand with Him and help children in their learning!

For Assignment and Discussion

1. Can you teach a child to be reverent better through precept or through imitation? Explain the method you would use.

2. According to the laws of learning, what is the best way to teach the Bible verse, "Love one another"?

3. In studying the different ways children learn, do you discover that any one of them has been neglected in your teaching?

4. Give a word picture of any learning experience on the part of a little child or a group of children. Note the ways of learning which entered into this experience.

Helpful Books

Understanding Children, Chapters V and VI, Sherrill
A Study of Young Children, Strang
Children Know Their Friends, Chapters I and II, Washburn
The Children We Teach, Chapter III, Whitehouse

---

[3] The teacher's part in the learning experiences of children will be treated further in chapter 4.

A Group of Kindergarten Children

If I had seen Thee, Master,
  With children on Thy knee,
And heard Thy loving accents,
  "Let children come to me,"
I think the inspiration
  Would last through all my days:
I'd speak, they'd follow after;
  They'd speak, I'd walk their ways.
O Master, fill my being
  With grace that comes from Thee;
And draw my little children
  To Thyself through me.

The Group

The children in the Kindergarten group are approximately four and five years of age, but the basis of grading should not be age alone. A child should be placed in the church school in the group of children whose development and interests are in line with his development and interests, in order that he may work happily and worship sincerely with them.

After a child in the Nursery Department has passed his fourth birthday, he is, if normally developed, ready for the Kindergarten. Some leaders think it wise to promote these children in a group on the first Promotion Day following the fourth birthday. Some recommend that they enter the Kindergarten individually as the birthday is reached, feeling that they may be more easily "absorbed" by the Kindergarten group. Still others find it better to promote these Nursery children once a quarter—perhaps the first Sunday of the quarter after they have become four. When this is done, usually several children enter the Kindergarten together and they feel more at home in the new situation because they have some of their own friends with them.

A warning is sometimes necessary against the practice of bringing Nursery children into the Kindergarten before they are four years of age. A period of a few weeks, at this age, is an important consideration.

An important factor to be taken into account in the best grouping of children is the public school grouping, in case the public school includes a kindergarten. Note the development of the children who attend the public school kindergarten. Church schools situated in communities where children do not enter the first grade in the public school at six years should take this into consideration when promoting.

The question sometimes arises, "What shall we do with the six-year-old child who has not had any public school experience?" In many cases this child will be more at home in the Kindergarten group, but there can be no hard and fast rule. Watch his social responses and carefully observe his development in skills, and place him where he will be happiest.

Standards of Promotion

As a rule, Kindergarten children are promoted to the Primary Department in a group. Our thinking on whether or not a child is ready for the Primary Department should be influenced by a combination of different evidences of development, such as age, knowledge, skills, and social adjustments.

Certainly knowledge alone should not qualify a child for promotion. The ability to repeat certain Bible verses and tell certain stories is not a safe measuring rod of achievement. But knowledge does have its place, in that it affects skills and social adjustments and all conduct. It is, therefore, desirable that the children should know and love certain Bible stories and verses and songs related to what they are thinking and doing.

Certain skills, such as the ability to read and write, will

have to play an important part in promotion later, but in the case of a Kindergarten child his happy adjustment to the group and its activities does not depend on such skills.

If it were possible to select a few of the most indicative bases of measuring the development of a Kindergarten child, such achievements as the ability to take care of belongings, the ability to follow directions reasonably well (both individual and group directions), and an evidenced desire to cooperate with other children in work and play enterprises, would probably be the ones chosen. Even so, these are hardly a measure of Christian attitudes and conduct.

A reasonably safe rule to follow is to promote the children of average development and proper social adjustment, who are around six years of age and who have just recently entered first grade of public school or will enter first grade within three or four months of the annual Promotion Day.

The Number in a Kindergarten

There was a time when a Kindergarten superintendent was wont to say rather proudly, "I have fifty children in my department!" Now, if she makes this statement, she makes it apologetically, for she realizes that no teacher can do informal work with a group of fifty children or help adequately in their development.[1]

The ideal number in a Kindergarten group is from twelve to twenty-five children. There should be enough children for social contacts and chances for living together and yet there should not be so many that the individual is lost in the group and has no chance for individual development.

When the group begins to number more than twenty-five children, it is time to think of the possibility of finding or building another room with a view to dividing the group into two groups or departments. Some churches, which have available rooms and enough leadership to warrant a division, closely grade the Kindergarten children into two depart-

---

[1] It is of interest to read in Edersheim's *In the Days of Christ* that "more than twenty-five pupils or thereabouts a schoolmaster was not allowed to teach in a class."

ments—the four-year-olds and the five-year-olds. This is a wise move, for there is a decided difference between children of these two ages in their attention spans and their ability to think and reason for themselves. The teacher who has tried to capture the attention of the new fours who have recently come from the Nursery and at the same time hold the interest of the ones almost six, knows what a hard job it is. It is much easier for the teachers to have the two ages separated and to plan according to the abilities of the different groups.

Other churches suggest subdividing the large department into small classes. This practice is not recommended. Often there are times when the children may arrange themselves in small informal groups for occasional activities, such as drawing, painting, pasting; looking at pictures or picture books, bird's nests or other objects; and engaging in conversation related to their activities. But, even in large departments, there should be a sense of unity in these activities that take place in the same room. There should be a time when the leader sits down with the whole group to tell a story, or engage in conversation or planning in which all are interested, to sing songs, or play games. The number in a group will greatly influence the leader in her plans for grouping. She should think first of the desired outcomes for which she is striving, and then decide which activities can best be developed in the group as a whole, which can best be developed in small groups under the leadership of assistants, and which lend themselves to individual participation. We often make the mistake of falling into a set method of grouping, without realizing that no one plan will suit every situation. The activities of one week may lend themselves to one method, while our purpose may best be accomplished the next week by an entirely different plan.

Where a Kindergarten is too large for informal learning, and where it is not possible for the church to find two available rooms which make possible a division into two groups, the same room may be used at different times by each group. In this case one group meets during the church school hour and the other during the hour for morning worship. In making such a division, the convenience of the parents should be taken into account, as the hour for adult worship will be much more convenient for some, while the church school hour will be the choice of others. There is, in most cases, no reason why each may not have a choice. However, if such a plan is followed, each of these groups should be kept separate and the children should not be allowed to change back and forth between groups. Such shifting might give a feeling of insecurity and instability to the children as well as work hardships on the teachers and handicap the leaders in providing for the best learning situations for the children.

Characteristics of Kindergarten Children

Each one of the children in a Kindergarten group is different because of his inherited tendencies, his physical make-up, and the special environment in which he lives. And yet these children are alike in many ways because they have lived through many similar experiences and their patterns of growth have been similar. Some of the general characteristics of Kindergarten children are considered here briefly.

Activity

The Kindergarten child is constantly active. It is the way God made him. He is still acquiring control over his large muscles, and most children of this age are not yet ready for small muscle control. He must be on the "go" and should not be expected to sit still for any length of time.

This need for activity should be taken into consideration by the teachers in setting up the room and in planning the procedures to be followed.

Curiosity

The Kindergarten child is curious and eager to know about things. He is continuously asking questions—Why? Where? How? He is exploring and experimenting, for that is one of the ways he learns.

The teacher may make use of this curiosity as she answers his questions and stimulates his interest in many things. This curiosity will often lead to wonder and this in turn may be guided to a moment of worship, as the child asks about the stars, or growing flowers, or other things, and the teacher by her answer may help him to feel close to God.

The following account is an illustration of how children were led from curiosity to worship on two different Sundays.

The children had planted some bulbs in bowls of moss one Sunday and were very much excited to find that some green shoots were visible the next Sunday. As they gathered around the table to look, one child asked, "How can those green leaves come out of that old brown thing we planted?" and before the teacher could answer, another said, "But those green things don't look like leaves." (The shoots were long and slender.) The teacher got another bulb which had not been planted and passed it around for the children to see and handle, so that all might remember what the bulbs looked like. Then they talked about how God planned that bulbs should have life in them even though they looked like "old brown things" and that when they were planted in the right way and watered, they started to grow. The group discussed the "green things that don't look like leaves"—how the leaves from bulbs are different from the leaves on bushes and trees. The children were very interested in this thought and by their questions and answers showed they were doing some real thinking along this line.

As they were showing evidences of wonder, the teacher said, "Isn't it wonderful that different bulbs and plants and trees all have different kinds of leaves? God planned it that way." There was a moment of silence and then one child remarked, "God is wonderful, Himself." The teacher answered, "Yes, He is. Let's tell Him how glad we are that He planned that bulbs should grow and that different plants should have different kinds of leaves." As the heads bowed, she voiced a simple prayer.

Two Sundays later the teachers forgot to bring the bowls of bulbs into the room. (They were placed outside in the sunshine through the week.) During the time when all of the children were in a group together, one of the boys remembered about the bulbs. So he and a helper went to bring them in. To their surprise two of the hyacinths (blue and pink) and one narcissus (white) were in bloom. There were squeals of delight when the children saw them and they rushed up to the table where the bowls were placed. There were many comments. "They are so pretty." "I like the pink one." "I like the blue one." They were all so happy about them that the teacher asked, "Shall we tell God how glad we are that the bulbs have bloomed?"

Several children bowed their heads and before the teacher could say anything, two spoke their thanks out loud to God.

Then the teacher spoke of the different colors and the different forms of the flowers (hyacinth and narcissus), and to stimulate their thinking she asked, "Do you remember that all the bulbs looked alike when we planted them? Do the flowers look alike now?" A chorus of "No" was followed by a moment of wonder as the children thought about this, and then one girl asked, "But how can they have different flowers?" The teacher answered, "Because that is the way God planned for it to be. Hyacinth bulbs always have hyacinth flowers and narcissus bulbs have narcissus flowers and rose bushes have roses. Aren't you glad that God planned it to be that way?" Many heads nodded and one child said softly, "Let's say 'Thank you' to God." And they did.

Love of Play

The Kindergarten child lives and learns through play. Play is actually his life, and it consists of all the busy, happy activities he is concerned with throughout his day.

When he joins a group, as in the church school, the four-year-old is inclined to play alone at first but enjoys the companionship of several others around him. As he becomes five, he participates more and more in co-operative play and is learning to understand the rights and feelings of others.

The teacher can use this love of play to help the child develop the Christian traits of kindness and friendliness.

Johnny is building a farm with the blocks. He wants some animals to place within the block fences. He sees that Jim has some animals and he goes over and grabs some of them. Jim immediately tries to snatch them back. The teacher approaches. She talks to both the boys, suggesting to Johnny that he should have asked Jim if he might play with some of the animals and suggesting to Jim that he might share some of the animals since he has so many. She explains that this is the way friends play together, sharing things, and then both are happy. Perhaps she will remind them that God wants children to be friendly and that the Bible says, "Be kind to one another." After a few moments Johnny asks Jim if he may have some of the animals for his farm and Jim hands him several. Both boys have made a step upward along the road of Christian living.

Joan is visiting in the Kindergarten. She does not know anyone and retreats to a corner refusing to do anything. One of the teachers speaks to Susan, suggesting that perhaps Joan will play with her if Susan asks her and hands her a doll. So Susan picks up a doll and, giving it to Joan, says, "Come on and let's play house." And in a few minutes Joan is happily engaged in playing house with the others. Susan has had the opportunity of learning to be friendly with a stranger and Joan has had the experience of someone being kind to her and of responding to that kindness—all through the medium of play.

Imagination

The Kindergarten child has a vivid imagination. This is shown in his play as he impersonates people, animals, and anything that comes to his mind. "Make believe" is a large part of his playing experiences.

It is through this imaginative play that a child lives his experiences and makes them a part of himself. As he plays, he really feels he is a daddy or a mother or a policeman, and his conduct as he plays the part shows the teacher what he thinks and feels. Often the teacher needs to direct this imaginative play along constructive instead of destructive lines.

Bobby was playing policeman and as he entered more and more into the role, he suddenly started to grab a boy who was playing with the blocks and shouted, "I'm taking you to jail!" And when the boy resisted he tried to knock him down. The teacher intervened and suggested other things policemen do. Before long Bobby was directing traffic and helping several "lost" children to find their homes.

Sometimes a child will become quite destructive as he plays with a truck, knocking it into block houses that others have built. The teacher may suggest something that his truck might carry, such as milk bottles, and direct his imagination along other lines where he would play more carefully.

He also can tell some rather fanciful tales. The four-year-old usually believes these wild stories he makes up, but the five-year-old is beginning to distinguish between truth and fancy.

The teacher does not want to stifle this God-given gift, but she does need to try to direct it along right channels. Often when a child has told an impossible tale as fact, the teacher may say, "You can make up nice stories. I sometimes make up stories to tell you, too. You like to hear the stories I make up for you and I like to hear your stories." If the teacher accepts his tales as "made-up" stories, although he declares them to be true ones, he soon will acknowledge them as "made up" also. Of course the teacher should be sure that the tales are fancy rather than fact, for sometimes fact is stranger than fiction.

There are times when a child may use too much imagination in a conversation about things he can do. For instance, a group was talking about helping at home and one five-year-old girl told of doing the whole family washing by herself. Instead of passing by the remark, the teacher said, "Ruth, I am sure you want to help Mother, and you can do all the washing when you get older. But right now you are five years old. Think of a way you can really help Mother now." After a moment, Ruth said, "Well, I can hand her the clothespins when she hangs up the clothes."

Imitation

The Kindergarten child is naturally imitative. Imagination and imitation are closely related in his play. Perhaps he has seen a motor boat going down the river—he finds a large box which his imagination immediately converts into a boat and he sits in it and imitates the actions of the driver as he "speeds down the river." He is constantly imitating the actions and the attitudes of the adults as well as the children around him.

His teachers and parents need to watch themselves closely to be sure they are worthy of his imitation.

Short Attention Span

The Kindergarten child is not able to concentrate for a very long period of time. Of course children differ in their powers of concentration, but most four- and five-year-old children have an interest span of about five minutes—often less. The four-year-old shifts his ideas frequently—the building he is making with blocks will change names many times in a few minutes of play, and his drawing or painting may start out to be a person but end up as a wagon. The five-year-old is more apt to have definite ideas in mind before starting his work and will usually stick to those ideas. However, neither age can be expected to remain too long with any one activity, although they can concentrate much longer on doing things than they can on listening or talking.

The teacher needs to keep this in mind as she plans her program, and to see that there are many varied activities in the sessions and that no one thing takes too long a time.

Limited Vocabulary

Although the Kindergarten child has a vocabulary of around two thousand words, he uses many words he does not understand. He is a great talker and enjoys using words, trying them out and inventing new ones. Many adults think these four-and five-year-old children understand because they are repeating the words exactly, but often it is only the sounds they are repeating and the words themselves have no meaning for them; and often they do not even get the sounds right.

One five-year-old came home from a public school kindergarten and announced, "We've learned a new long prayer. It's called 'The Lost Prayer.'" (This proved to be the Lord's Prayer.) The mother was rather worried, for she knew a five-year-old could not possibly understand the meanings in this prayer and this was borne out as the child glibly recited it. When she came to the phrase, "Forgive us our trespasses," she said, "Forgive us our Christmases as we forgive those who Christmas against us."

These children cannot understand abstract or symbolical terms. They are imaginative and impersonate people and things, but they do this only in concrete ways. A four-year-old mother will take her imaginary children out for a walk, or rock them to sleep in such a natural manner that they must be very real to her. But this same child, at the suggestion of "being a sunbeam for Jesus," will think only of *literal* sunbeams. The teacher must remember this and strive to use only simple words that four- and five-year-old children can understand.

Limited Understanding of Adult Ways

The Kindergarten child has so much to learn in this world of adults. He is encouraged to mark with crayons, but it must be on certain paper and not on the walls. One day an adult smiles when he does something when other people are present; the next day the same adult frowns when he does the same thing when they are alone. He is urged to feed himself (at the table), but if he opens the refrigerator to take something to feed himself, it is a different matter. Often the polite statement of an adult sounds to him like an untruth. Sometimes behavior which is condoned at home cannot be allowed in the church school group.

The teacher needs to try to put herself in the child's place, look at surroundings and actions through the child's eyes, so that she may better understand him.

Limited Understanding of Time, Distance, and Numbers

The Kindergarten child has little sense of time. The words "tomorrow" and "yesterday" have little meaning for him. But if those words can be related to something he does remember, he will understand; for instance—"Yesterday when we went to Grandmother's," or "Tomorrow, after you go to bed tonight and wake up in the morning."

Distance and numbers also have little meaning for this age unless related to his immediate experiences. "A mile" means nothing, but "as far as from here to the church" gives him an idea he can grasp. He can comprehend numbers up through six and perhaps ten, but large numbers are beyond him, although he loves to use them.

The teacher must be careful as she talks with these children to try to relate her words to things they can understand—things that are within their experiences.

Individual Characteristics

As these general characteristics are considered, the teacher must not lose sight of the special needs of individual children.

There may be a four-year-old in the group who is quite immature—perhaps this child has been sick much of his life and has had no experiences with other children. Allowances will have to be made for such a child. It may be necessary for him to play alone even when the others join in whole group activities, until the time comes when he has matured enough to take his place in the group with the others.

There may be a child in the class who seems to be older than the other children. Special plans will have to be made for him so he will not be bored or become bossy with the others. He can be given special duties to perform. Perhaps he can be guided to see ways in which he can help the younger ones. Perhaps at times he might be asked to recall one of the stories. His abilities, as one of the older ones, should be recognized and he should be made to feel that he is a helper and is needed in the group.

So a Kindergarten group comes together on a Sunday morning—a group of active, curious, imaginative children, who cannot concentrate long at a time, who often do not understand the teacher's words or ideas, but who love to play and to imitate and who are eager to learn. The teacher sees all their similarities but she also tries to see each child individually, and she plans ways and means of guiding each one from where he now is to a fuller, richer life that God would have him live.

For Assignment and Discussion

1. From the study of the Kindergarten children in your group, what general characteristics could you add to the list given in this chapter?

2. Choose five children from your group and mention ways in which they differ from each other.

3. Give reasons for and against promoting children from the Nursery to the Kindergarten only once a year on Promotion Day.

4. How would you answer this plea of a teacher? "John is only

five years of age, but his playmates are, as a rule, boys older than he. He considers some of the things we do in Kindergarten 'babyish' and he is no longer interested. What shall we do with him?"

Helpful Books and Leaflets

Education in the Kindergarten, second edition, Chapter I, Foster and Headley

Living in the Kindergarten, Chapter II, Wills and Stegeman

The First Five Years of Life, Chapter IV, Gesell and others

Infant and Child in the Culture of Today, Chapters XIX and XX, Gesell and others

Teaching Kindergarten Children, Chapter I, Gardner

Portfolio for Kindergarten Teachers, Association for Childhood Education, Washington, D. C.

Denominational and interdenominational leaflets and pamphlets

The Leaders of a Kindergarten Group

A TEACHER OF RELIGION

How dare I name myself as one
　Who goes the way to God?
As one who knows and walks the path
　Devoted feet have trod?

I cannot name myself as one
　Who never goes astray—
Who never stumbles on the road,
　Or never leaves the way.

But, when I know that baby feet
　Will follow where I've trod,
I walk with care that they may keep
　The road that leads to God.

Number of Leaders Needed

For each Kindergarten group there should be a leading teacher and one or more assistants as needed. The number of assistants should be in about the proportion of one helper for each five or six children, including the secretary and pianist. For instance, in a group of twenty or twenty-five children there should be a leading teacher and four assistants. Of these, one may serve as secretary and one as pianist in addition to other teaching duties.

Even though the group is quite small, it is desirable to have both a leading teacher and an assistant. Emergencies often arise where it is necessary for a teacher to take a child away from the group because of sudden sickness or accident and the other children should not be left alone. Also there are times when the leader herself is sick and someone who is familiar with the children and the procedure should be there to take over.

Throughout this chapter (and the whole book) reference is made to the teachers as women, mainly because, at present, women seem to predominate as Kindergarten teachers and assistants. But this does not mean that there are no men Kindergarten teachers. More and more men are taking their places alongside the women in teaching children, and if they are good teachers, the children receive great benefit from the influence of men as well as women.

Qualifications and Characteristics of a Successful Kindergarten Leader

The terms "leader" and "teacher" are used interchangeably in this discussion.

1. This teacher should be a sincere Christian and have an intelligent and positive Christian faith.

The children will not understand that her acceptance of Jesus as Saviour and Lord makes her a better teacher, but they can understand that this person loves God, the heavenly Father, and Jesus Christ, His Son, and is trying to do the things which are pleasing to God. All of this will be felt intangibly by the children and is one of the great factors in influencing the lives of the children.

The faith of this teacher should be well thought out. Just because she is teaching young children and may have no occasion to state her faith to them in so many words is no reason why she should not be able to put her beliefs into words. This well-thought-out faith will be the foundation of her teaching.

This teacher should be one who understands religion on the Kindergarten child's level. This means, among other things, that: (a) she will understand what the religious needs of this age are and will try to meet those needs; (b) she will give to the child what he can understand and not try to force upon him things which are beyond his ability to grasp; (c) she will realize that play is a part of a child's life and religion—the part where he should be learning to get along with others in a Christian way; (d) she will know that the moments of worship at this age are fleeting and she must be ready to grasp them as they are presented.

2. This teacher should understand Kindergarten children.

She should know their basic needs and what can be done to meet those needs; she should know the general characteristics of this age; she should understand how these children grow and develop and how they learn, how their abilities and limitations compare with the ages preceding and following this age. It is only with such a knowledge and understanding that she will be able to guide the children through all their experiences toward the goals of Christian education.

3. This teacher should have a growing knowledge of the content and message of the Bible.

She will not impart much of this knowledge directly to the children, but it will give her a background so that she will have a clearer picture of Bible history, times, and customs and a better understanding of the passages which are suggested for her own use and for use with the children. She will make great strides in her own spiritual development as she studies the Word of God.

She should have a deep sense of the value of the Bible for our times today. The Bible should be her guide for Christian living and she should make constant use of it as she accepts its teachings as the rules for her living and as the foundation for her philosophy of life.

She also should understand what Biblical material is suitable for this age child. The material used, stories and verses, should be both understandable and of value to the child for the living of his life now, rather than for storing it up in his memory in the hope that it may be of use at a later time.

4. This teacher should have an interest in and love for children.

This is not the gushing sort of "love" expressed by some people in a statement such as, "Aren't these little dears cute!

I just love them!" Neither is it the kind of love that smothers and coddles. The Kindergarten teacher should have a genuine love for children, individually as well as collectively. She should like them whether they are good or bad, whether they are clean or dirty, whether they are dressed up or in rags. She should have a real interest in them, in their individual needs, in their limitations and their abilities, and she should have a desire to help each child in every possible way.

5. This teacher should take time to study and improve her work.

She should study to understand the characteristics of this age of children, the laws of learning and the ways of teaching. She should read books and magazines containing helps for her task, trying to apply what she reads. She should attend all available leadership education courses which will help her in her own spiritual growth and knowledge and in her teaching work. Thus she will be a growing person—one who is studying to present herself "to God as one approved, a workman who has no need to be ashamed." (II Timothy 2:15, r.s.v.)

6. This teacher should have a friendly and courteous attitude toward the children as well as toward adults.

A genuine friendliness cannot be counterfeited. Each child should feel, "When something happens, I want to tell my teacher about it, for she is my friend." The teacher's thoughtful, impartial friendliness is big enough to embrace every child in the group. She is really interested in Jack's new coat, Joe's stumped toe, and Carol's new brother. Her courtesy dignifies the concerns of the children and accords the same consideration to them which would be expected and received by adults.

7. This teacher should have a happy spirit.

She should radiate joy and good cheer—this makes her attractive to children, and they quickly catch her spirit.

A group of Juniors was once asked to think back over all

the teachers they had had and to name the one they liked the best and tell the reason for the choice. One boy named his Kindergarten teacher because, he said, "She was always happy and her eyes were always smiling."

8. This teacher should have a pleasant voice.

A high-pitched strident voice will add tension to any group; while a calm, low voice will have a soothing effect on the children. However, this calm, low voice must be strong enough to be heard by all the children, for those who cannot hear cannot be expected to listen. A pleasing voice can be cultivated through practice and vigilance.

9. This teacher should be calm and patient.

A flurried, hurried teacher has no place in the Kindergarten. Children so quickly catch and react to nervousness or uncertainty that it takes only a few minutes for a nervous teacher to find she is teaching nervous children.

This teacher should be willing to give the boys and girls time to do things at their own pace; she should wait patiently for a child to handle a picture or adjust his words or find his money or put the flowers in a vase. She should be willing to allow the children to grow and develop at their own rate.

Calmness and patience can be acquired through persistent effort and prayer and are certainly worth the striving it takes to attain them.

10. This teacher should be open-minded.

Dr. Vieth says, in speaking of the experimental attitude: "If a modern Solomon were to utter the prayer of his deepest desire, he would do well to add to his petition for an understanding heart a request for an open mind. And if he were to become a teacher in the church school he would need a double portion of this blessing. . . . Christian convictions may be the same from age to age, but they must be applied to conditions which are ever new in a changing world. Our purpose with and for children may be the same today as yesterday, but our manner of dealing with children must change with the increase of knowledge of how learning takes place."[1]

The teacher should be willing to try new methods and new activities, studying them, giving them a fair trial, and evaluating the results.

11. This teacher should be dependable.

She should be regular in her attendance at the church school. She should be prepared for her part in the session procedures. She should keep her promises to the children and to adults. Her children should know that they can count on her at all times.

In addition to these qualifications, the leading teacher should have the background and ability:

1. To provide the right kind of teaching experiences for the children.

She should be able to plan activities through which she can lead the children into experiences of learning. If she desires to teach them to play happily together, she will plan for actual playtimes when she will guide them in their activity. If she wants them to feel a love and reverence for the church, she will take them softly into the church auditorium at a time when perhaps only the minister is there. These experiences foster learning.

She should be able to grasp suggestions of the children themselves and turn them into teaching opportunities. An example of this is found in the account of the session in Chapter I when the teacher took the group outside to see the real bird nest which one child had discovered instead of keeping to her original plan of showing a last year's nest.

The teacher should be able and ready to supply information when needed and try to answer questions with real wisdom. This means she will have to know how to translate her information into terms that a young child can understand. She must know also how to say frankly at times, "That is something I do not know," or "There are some things that no one but God knows."

---

[1] Vieth, *Teaching for Christian Living*. Bethany Press. Used by permission.

2. To promote good relationships in the department.

She needs those qualities of spirit and joyfulness in her task which promote good feelings between her fellow teachers, as well as between teachers and pupils. She needs to be able to inspire her workers with the privileges that are theirs of bringing children closer to God.

She needs good administrative ability which will insure the smooth running of the department. This will be discussed under the topic on the work of the leading teacher.

3. To promote good relationships with the home.

This leading teacher should have the qualities that make for good parent-teacher relationships. She should be frank when the occasion demands it, but at the same time tactful, thinking of the point of view of the parent and of the child. She should be careful of her words. She should be friendly. She should be trustworthy—able to keep confidences.

This leading teacher should be mature enough for parents to respect her judgment, and she should have enough common sense mingled with knowledge and with actual experience to cause parents to want to seek her judgment concerning their children. The teacher who is able to talk sanely and wisely with the parents is often able to help them get a new light on the problems of their children.

The Work of Department Leaders

In the following discussions the terms "superintendent-teacher" and "leading teacher" are used interchangeably.

THE WORK OF THE SUPERINTENDENT-TEACHER OR LEADING TEACHER

1. The superintendent-teacher is responsible for the organization and administration of the department.

Whether the department or group be large or small, there are many definite duties which have to be attended to in order that things may go smoothly, and it is the responsibility of the superintendent-teacher to see that these duties are done by herself or others. In other words, she is responsible for the "well-being" of the department.

2. It is the responsibility of the superintendent-teacher to see that the right teaching materials are used in the department.

These materials should be the ones selected by the Committee on Christian Education or other responsible group in the church.

3. The superintendent-teacher should arrange for and delegate responsibilities for the age-group planning meetings.

She should arrange for the meetings of all the assistants where they will plan together for the next unit of work. She should see that the leader's guides have been placed in the hands of the assistants prior to this meeting and should encourage them to study these guides. She should be instrumental in mapping out what should be done at the meeting and assign any special reports to the assistants. Before the meeting she should carefully study the leader's guide and plan any adaptations of material she feels should be made. These would be subject to change when discussed with the helpers at the meeting. A section of this chapter gives more information about these planning meetings.

4. The superintendent-teacher should make clear to the assistants their responsibilities in the session activities.

She should be sure that each worker understands what was delegated to her at the planning meeting. If any helper was not present at that meeting, the leading teacher should talk over with her the responsibilities assigned to her. When an assistant notifies the superintendent-teacher that she cannot be present on Sunday, it is the responsibility of the superintendent-teacher to assign that person's duties to one of the other workers.

The leading teacher should guide the assistants to learn to watch for opportunities when special help is needed by the children. She should show appreciation of evidences of good judgment on the part of a helper by a tactful word of praise, sometimes given in the presence of other helpers. She should give constructive criticism tactfully, and if she invites her helpers to criticize her own mistakes, it will make for an atmosphere of give and take which will develop in both leader and helpers the power of self-criticism.

5. The superintendent-teacher is responsible, usually, for the large group activities in the session.

This will be that part of the procedure where the children all come together for conversation, singing, hearing a story, worship, and such activities; and usually the leading teacher is responsible for guiding the children at this time.

6. The superintendent-teacher will develop leadership by using assistants sometimes to lead the large group activities.

At times she will delegate to some of her assistants the responsibility of telling a story or introducing a song, or leading a conversation or guiding a game activity, in order that these assistants may learn to become leaders.

7. The superintendent-teacher is responsible for keeping the session activities integrated and unified.

These activities will have been planned in the planning meeting, but the leading teacher will be the one to decide that perhaps some activity, which is being enjoyed by the children and is helping them in a special way, will be continued for a longer time, and that some other activity will have to be cut short or excluded.

Also she will be the one who will unify all the activities of the session if some of the helpers are taking part in leading the large group. It is her job to be the person who is in charge, to gather up any loose ends and to keep things going, even though the story or songs or other activities may be led by others.

8. The superintendent-teacher should arrive early on Sunday and work with the assistants in preparation for the session.

All of the workers need to be sure that everything is in readiness for the activities of the day. The leader who rushes in late, out of breath and nervous, cannot expect to guide a calm and receptive group of children. Her manner will be reflected in their responses.

9. The superintendent-teacher should keep in touch with the homes of the children in the department.

It is very important that she know the children and their family backgrounds. The best way she can do this is by visiting in the homes. This will help her to make friends with the parents and the children, and will give her aid in understanding the causes underlying many problems.

The parents should be kept informed of the plans for the children and should co-operate in making many of these plans. Parent-sponsors may be appointed to help in this task. The work of the parent-sponsors and suggestions for parent-teacher relationships will be found in Chapter XII.

10. The superintendent-teacher should take advantage of opportunities for leadership education for the assistants and for herself.

Whenever courses in leadership education are offered, the superintendent-teacher should try to take such courses and urge her assistants to enroll also. She should provide magazines and books in the field of religious education and call the attention of her assistants to special articles or chapters. At times she should allow her helpers to visit in other schools and then ask them to report back to the others for discussion any special activities or ways of teaching which they observed. She should hold before her assistants the importance of continually studying and improving their work.

11. The superintendent-teacher will co-operate in general Workers' Conferences and any meetings where her children or her leaders are involved.

The Kindergarten is a part of the whole church school and it is very necessary that the superintendent-teacher and her assistants attend and take part in the general Workers' Conference where all plans and procedures are inaugurated in the light of the knowledge of what other departments are doing. They should also attend and co-operate in any other meetings which concern children or religious education. The workers in a Kindergarten should take their places in such conferences or meetings, make their contributions, gain the inspiration that comes from an appreciation of the work of others, and experience the joy of co-operation.

12. The superintendent-teacher should recommend to the Committee on Christian Education suitable persons to serve as assistants.

She should be constantly on the lookout for understanding young women or men who are potential leaders of young children. After prayerful consideration of these people, she should submit their names to the Committee on Christian Education or other responsible group in the church for consideration as assistants in the Kindergarten Department. These people should be invited to take a training class and then join the department, perhaps as apprentice teachers, to continue their training under the supervision of the superintendent-teacher.

THE WORK OF THE ASSISTANTS

1. The assistants should arrive early and be ready to guide the children in early activities.

This is especially needful for the leading teacher, the secretary, and the pianist, but it is also important to have every helper in her place before any of the children arrive. The late helper does not always know that she has caused a last-minute change in plans—often a change that has caused the children to suffer. The workers should be ready to guide the children in any activities which have been planned for the early comers.

2. The assistants should assume responsibility in helping to keep the room orderly.

Upon arrival, each helper should remove her hat and coat, placing them and her pocketbook in the spot provided for them—never on top of the piano!

As the children arrive, the assistants should see that they put their hats and coats in the proper place. This does not mean that the helpers should do this for them. The children should be encouraged to do all they can for themselves. This is part of their training in self-reliance.

The room should always be set up in a neat and orderly fashion before any of the children arrive, but the early comers may help in placing the pictures on the picture rail or board, assist in fixing the flowers, putting out the offering basket and Bible on the worship or beauty center, placing the music books on the piano, and other simple things which have to be done each Sunday. The assistants should supervise the doing of such things by the children.

Throughout the session the helpers should remind the children to put away things which they have finished using and should help the children do this.

3. The assistants should be prepared to guide the activities of small groups.

During the playtime, an assistant may quietly join a group at play or a group at a loss as to what to play, and without dominating she may tactfully lead them into worth-while activity. She may help the children procure certain play materials that suggest an activity. She may play with them, helping to connect the play with familiar teaching content —as with a story, a song, or conversation which relates to the play. In other words, a skillful assistant will help to make free play happy and meaningful.

The children who are engaged in work activities should be divided into small groups, each under the guidance of one of the helpers. This helper is not to do the work for any of the children, but encourage each child to do his own work in a creative way. The adult who takes the materials away from the child and does it herself because she cannot stand to see the child "mess it up" is harming the child in more ways than one. She is keeping the child from becoming self-reliant; she is helping him to become frustrated; she may be teaching the child deception if others think he did the work; and it is certainly not wholesome for him to know that the other children worked for their results while he put forth no effort.

Occasionally the children will be divided into small groups for conversation or recalling stories or looking at pictures or such activities, and an assistant will be in charge of each group, and should be prepared to lead this group carefully in whatever activity is planned.

If a helper overhears a conversation that throws light upon the behavior of certain children, or if she observes any unusual behavior, she should make a mental note of it to share it with the other teachers after the session or at the next planning meeting.

4. The assistants should help set the room in order for further activities.

The teachers will help the children put away toys and materials when the play or work times are finished, and will move chairs and tables if this is necessary for the making of the semicircle for the large group activities or any other activities.

5. The assistants should watch for opportunities to give special help when it is needed, but be careful not to intrude unless it is necessary.

When the children are called together in the large group, each assistant will find a place in the semicircle of children. She will try to sit near any child whom she sees may require some supervision or one who may need comforting. Then, as the leading teacher conducts the activities of the group, the helper will enter into the activities just as the children do, for the children will imitate her actions and attitudes. As she does this, however, she will be constantly watching both the children and the leading teacher. Perhaps it will be necessary for her to place a gentle restraining hand on the shoulder of a child who is bothering other children, or she may catch a nod from the teacher that someone needs to be taken to the bathroom.

Sometimes it takes quick judgment to decide whether to intrude or not. For instance, Lucy begins to cry just as the leading teacher starts to tell a story. Will Lucy stop crying in time to keep from spoiling the story, or should the helper take her on her lap, or should she quietly persuade her to go outside the room where she will not disturb the whole group?

The assistants should be keen and wide-awake to the needs of all the children during all the session, whether it be during large or small group activities or during free play. Each can keep a watchful eye on the children nearest her and keep tuned to the leading teacher for looks of guidance.

6. The assistants should accept assignments for and attend all planning conferences.

Every helper should attend the unit planning meetings of the department. She should take her turn in giving the devotional or special reports to the group. She should read all the suggestions in the leader's manual for the unit and be prepared to help talk about adapting these suggestions to fit the local situation. She should accept duties and responsibilities assigned to her at this meeting and keep a written record of all duties so assigned.

7. The assistants should always notify the superintendent-teacher of any proposed absences.

As soon as an assistant knows she will not be able to be present at any session or at a planning meeting, she should notify the leading teacher. This is very important in order that the work of the department may go smoothly.

8. The assistants should assume responsibility for any advance preparation of materials before the session.

Perhaps certain objects or pictures are needed for the session; or it may be that pictures need to be mounted; perhaps materials should be prepared for certain creative activities. All such things should be done before the session, and the responsibility for doing these should be assumed by the assistants at the planning meeting.

9. At times, the assistants should take specific teaching assignments in the large group.

It is only as the helpers are willing to take actual teaching assignments when the leader asks them, that they can learn how to teach. So, at times, they should try telling a story, leading a conversation, introducing a song, or guiding other activities for the whole group.

10. The secretary-treasurer has special duties.

In addition to helping with the children, the secretary-treasurer should keep all the attendance records and an account of all money received and disbursed. She may also act as a hostess, meeting the children and any adult visitors and quietly welcoming them. She should do any writing that needs to be done, and send, at the request of the superintendent, all necessary letters for the department. She sometimes needs to be cautioned not to let these mechanical duties interfere with her responsibility as a contributor to the general atmosphere of the department.

If the group is very large, the secretary should not be expected to enter into the activities with the children, as her time will be completely taken up during the session with welcoming and dismissing the children and their parents, checking the roll and offering, seeing that materials are laid out for any creative work, taking care of the current pupil material, and doing the many other duties which belong in her realm.

Her special tasks would also include estimating the number of teachers' helps and pupil material, with the superintendent-teacher's approval, in order that such a list may be included in the general order of the church school. When the supplies arrive, she should sort them out and put them in the place specially assigned for them.

11. The pianist has special duties.

In addition to helping with the children as the other assistants do, the pianist will play for the songs, rhythms, and other activities. Her special work is discussed near the end of Chapter IX.

Planning Meetings

In order for the work in the group or department to run smoothly, all who teach or help must plan together. If there are parent sponsors, they should be on hand. Such planning meetings should be held before each unit begins. Some time before the meeting each worker should be given a copy of the leader's guide and the pupil's material, and each one should read carefully all the material related to the unit to be used. At the meeting there should be time for inspiration, information, discussion, planning, and fellowship.

The leading teacher will conduct the meeting somewhat as follows:

Devotional. This might be based upon the Bible verses that will be used by the children during the month. It should be assigned to someone beforehand.

Report of a book or article or something especially helpful to the teachers. This should also be assigned beforehand to one of the assistants.

Announcements.

Short evaluation of past unit or of children's conduct.

Discussion of unit purpose.

Choosing special activities from those suggested in the leader's manual or by some of the workers.

Making detailed plans for each session and adapting plans suggested in leader's guide.

Assigning responsibilities for various duties and activities.

Learning new songs.

Closing prayer.

Short time for fellowship.

If the group of children is so small that there is only one teacher, she should, if possible, have one of the parents act as parent sponsor. (See Chapter XII.) This person would plan with her and then would be able to take over in case of an emergency. Whether there be only one or ten teachers, practically the same procedure of planning as suggested above can be followed.

It is very important that these planning meetings be held, and it is also very important that every teacher attend them and keep notes, so that each one will know exactly what her duties and responsibilities are for every Sunday. It is only as all the workers co-operate that the children will be guided toward the goals which have been set for their Christian education.

Training for Leadership

Opportunities for study and training are always available to earnest students. There are current religious magazines, as well as helpful books, written out of the rich experiences of teachers of children.

One of the most worth-while opportunities for training is the Leadership Education class or school, made available by all of the denominations. In addition to the strictly denominational schools, there are interdenominational schools planned to meet the various situations in which teachers find themselves.

By far the most valuable means of training for leadership is the Laboratory School in which students are given opportunities for practice teaching under supervision. The usual procedure in such schools is to give a certain amount of time for the study of children and methods of working with them, an hour in the actual experience of a session with the children, and perhaps another hour in a discussion of the responses of the children, the successes and failures of the methods used, and a detailed arrangement for the next day's work.

Sometimes there are opportunities to observe good teaching in a neighboring church, possibly under the guidance of a teacher-consultant whose department is recognized as a training center.

For students who cannot do classwork or guided observation, there are correspondence courses. Those who are now teaching in the church school, and others who are hoping to teach, should communicate with their denominational headquarters for information about schools, classes, and the possibility of correspondence courses.

It is a joy and privilege to be a Kindergarten teacher; a joy and privilege to watch children grow in the love and knowledge of God and Jesus and in their ability to get along with others in a Christian way; a special joy and privilege to know that you, as the teacher, are serving in God's Kingdom.

For Assignment and Discussion

1. Discuss the following:
   Adult visitors.
   Assistants who are always late.
   Children who are always late.

2. If you are an assistant in a Kindergarten, list some of the ways you can do a better job of helping there. If you are the leading teacher, list some of the ways you can help your assistants do their work better.

3. Plan a year's program for your own spiritual and mental growth. Include leadership education, special studying, reading, etc.

Helpful Books and Pamphlets

Principles of Teaching and Learning in the Elementary School, Chapter XII, Mossman (out of print, may be available in your library)

Education in the Kindergarten, second edition, Chapter III, Foster and Headley

Heaven in My Hand, Humphreys

Angels in Pinafores, Humphreys

Denominational and interdenominational pamphlets

CHAPTER V

The Children's Room for Work and Play and Worship

Atmosphere

Perhaps you are walking in the cool of the evening when the lengthening shadows have almost melted into twilight. The sun has set, and dimming shafts of golden light are breaking through clouds of violet and rose. Through the lacy branches of arching trees an evening star is shining. The world seems very peaceful. God seems very near, and you remember that "the groves were God's first temples." It is easy for you to worship, for you are surrounded by an atmosphere of worship.

It is Sunday morning. Quietly you walk through an open Gothic doorway. The mellow morning light is filtering through the arching windows. Bells are chiming in the steeple and soft strains of music are filling the church as you take your seat. God seems very near, and you remember that He said, "My house shall be called a house of prayer." It is easy to worship, for you are surrounded by an atmosphere of worship.

Atmospheres really affect us, do they not?

Suppose you were a four- or five-year-old child. There are certain atmospheres which make it easy for you to realize that you are close to God. There are certain church school rooms in which you like to stay. Such a room might be described as follows.

A Room for Work and Play and Worship

The character of the room is felt the moment one enters the door. It has a warmth and a sense of having been used by children. The warmth comes perhaps from the walls, which are a soft, pale amber. The ceiling, not too high, is a lighter tone of this same color.

The woodwork, including the picture rail, is a deep ivory; the hardwood floor is light oak; the chairs and tables are a natural wood finish.

The rug on the floor is hard to describe. It is a mingling of the autumn colors—the golden brown, the russet, and the fading orange of leaves that have fallen—colors warm, but mellow and restful.

The curtains at the low, wide windows are a sunshiny shade of sheer cotton. Growing plants on a table near the window catch the morning sunshine.

A picture, Plockhorst's "Christ Blessing Little Children," is hung low at the front of the room. There are several large pictures on a low picture rail at one side of the room, where a group of children have gathered and are talking about the pictures with one of the assistant teachers.

In front of the picture, "Christ Blessing Little Children," is a low table on which is placed a Bible, a small offering basket, and a vase of beautiful flowers. This vase of flowers seems to catch and hold the light of the room. To one side is a low piano where several children have gathered to sing as a teacher plays for them.

Over on one side of the room is a long box containing blocks, and a group of children are busily engaged in building activities. Across the room is a housekeeping corner which contains a doll bed and dolls, a tea party table and dishes. Many of the children are playing there.

On one table toward the back of the room there are picture books lying invitingly open, and some treasures which the children have brought to share with others. At another table several boys and girls are seated happily drawing with crayons.

As any child enters this room it seems to call out invitingly, "Come and work and play and worship."

Building an Adequate Room

This word picture emphasizes the type of church school room in which Kindergarten children can best be taught in an informal way. Of course not all Kindergarten Departments can have an ideal setup, but since many churches are building new educational plants or remodeling, certain details in building are suggested which may be of help to the building committee and architect. The superintendents of departments should have ample opportunity to present their needs to the committee. It should be remembered that a building, in most cases, stands for a generation, and oftentimes longer. The decision as to what this building shall be is a serious responsibility.

Also the details given here may furnish suggestions to teachers as they try to renovate and fix over unattractive and poorly equipped rooms.

Size of the Room

The room should be large enough for all activities, and yet not so large that it will lose its homelike atmosphere. The accepted proportion is from twenty-five to thirty-five square feet for each child. A room planned for twenty children should contain *not less than* five hundred square feet of floor space.

In planning for more than twenty-five children there should be two Kindergarten rooms instead of one. In very large churches there may be a necessity for a number of departmental rooms. For example, if there are as many as sixty children they should be treated practically as three departments; and three rooms, each containing about five hundred or more square feet of floor space, should be provided.

The shape of the room is largely a matter of taste, but a room that is longer than it is wide lends itself to the activities of children better than a square room.

Openings

Good architects, of course, take into account the question of the proper lighting and ventilation of a room, but many forget or have never thought that the windows in a room to be used by little children should be low enough for the use of the children in case the outlook is at all desirable.[1] Clear glass is preferable to stained glass, unless the outlook is very undesirable. In this case a pale amber may be used. A safe estimate of the proportion of light needed is that the window space shall be at least 25 per cent of the floor space.

The position of the door may seem a trivial item, but the entrance of late comers or visitors may be disturbing if the door is in the wrong place. It should be in the back of the room where it will least interfere with the activities of the children.

Floors

The floor should be such that the children can play on it, therefore it must be smooth and easily cleaned. If it is hardwood, it should be free from splinters, waxed, but never oiled. It can be covered with asbestos tile, rubber tile, or inlaid linoleum in solid colors or simple marbleized patterns. A rug on which the children may sit during the story time will add to the homelike appearance of the room.

Built-in Cabinet

As it is certain that a cabinet will be needed, it is well to have it built in when the room is being constructed. This cabinet should be in the back of the room so that it may not prove a distraction. In addition to adequate space for various teaching materials to be handled by the teacher, it may contain low shelves for the use of the children, or these low shelves may be provided elsewhere in the room. It is also well to design this cabinet to provide a place for the teachers' wraps and personal belongings.

---

[1] Architects naturally object to putting low windows in one or two rooms only. For this reason a request for low windows should be made before plans are drawn, so that the whole plan may be made with them in mind.

On the upper shelves of the cabinet will be placed materials that will be handled first by the teachers, such as the Bible, pupils' material, large pictures, Manila paper, construction paper in assorted colors, paper napkins, large scissors, thumbtacks, paper clips, pins, Scotch tape, vases, dustcloths, newspapers, first aid kit, and nature specimens.

On the lower shelves will be placed materials to be handled and cared for directly by the children, such as picture books, pictures, Manila and construction paper, scissors (small with blunt points), large crayons, paste, twine, tempera paints and paint brushes (if these are to be used), and treasures brought by the children. Also if there are no other low shelves available in the room, the toys from the various play centers should be placed here.

File for Mounted Pictures

If the shelves of the cabinet are of the right size and there is enough storage space, the large pictures may be kept there. However, many teachers find that a large, deep box or bin is more satisfactory than open shelves, and may be planned carefully with reference to the size of the largest pictures used. Such a file makes it possible to locate pictures more quickly than on a shelf. Another means of filing these pictures is the use of the cardboard boxes containing the large X-ray films used by hospitals and laboratories. These are just the right size for the teaching pictures provided by the different denominations.

Picture Rail

Some provision for temporary pictures should be included in the plans for the room. Many schools are using a picture rail. This rail is similar to a plate rail. It should be grooved, and should extend six or eight inches from the wall. If placed about twenty-six inches from the floor, it will be easy to place mounted pictures within the vision of a little child. It should be fastened to the wall in the front of the room where the children will face it as they gather together in a semicircle for the group activities.

Display Space

A bulletin board is not necessary for a Kindergarten room, but the children do enjoy having a place where their drawings or the pictures they bring may be placed. If there is room, a piece of cork or beaverboard three or four feet long could be placed on one of the walls twelve to eighteen inches from the floor. Of course this necessitates the use of thumbtacks, which often presents a problem. A substitute for such a board is a wire stretched along a wall about thirty inches from the floor; on this the children can clip their drawings with small plastic clothespins.

Place for Wraps

There should be a convenient place for hanging the children's coats. Sometimes this is placed in a special coatroom adjoining the Kindergarten room, but often it is in the room itself. A movable screen with a low rail across the back for brackets on which a number of coat hangers may be hung is a space saver. A shelf for hats and pocketbooks may be built above the coatrack. The screen can serve a double purpose, as the back holds coats and hats, and the front may be used as a bulletin board for pictures and the children's drawings. A place for the teachers' wraps and purses should be provided also.

Toilet

A toilet should be located either just off the Kindergarten room or very near to it. The use of small low equipment in this room makes it convenient for the children.

Shelves

Low shelves where the children's books, toys, housekeeping and block building equipment may be kept should be provided if the cabinet does not have such space. These shelves should be open and built about fourteen or fifteen inches apart.

Color Combinations

In choosing the color scheme of any room, there are a few principles which should be kept in mind.

1. Walls should be treated as backgrounds, using soft neutral colors. Warm tones of yellow are best for dark rooms, while light shades of green or blue-green are better for rooms that tend to be bright.

2. The ceiling should usually be lighter in color than the walls, unless it is quite high.

3. The woodwork, including shelves and cabinet, should all be the same color. This should be the same color as the walls or harmonize with the walls.

4. A note of vivid color should be obtained in a vase or a picture or flowers, rather than in the permanent decorations.

Furnishings and Equipment

In choosing the furnishings for a Kindergarten room, the thought of durability should be taken into account, as well as the pleasing appearance of the furnishings. Sometimes it is more economical to buy the best in the beginning, rather than to face the necessity of renewal at frequent intervals.

Chairs for the Children

Strong, durable chairs are greatly to be desired, but they should be light enough in weight for the children to carry, and they must be comfortable. They should have backs which will be supports to fit the hollow of the backs of the children as well as supports for the shoulders. The seats should be made to fit the form of the child. These chairs should be either ten or twelve inches high.

Chairs for Visitors

There should be a few chairs for occasional visitors, placed at the back of the room, where they will not interfere with the spontaneity and naturalness of the children.

Tables for the Children

Low tables about twenty inches high, or ten inches higher than the chair seats, are desirable. They should be rectangular in shape because this type of table takes up less space and may be pushed back against the walls to give more room. The table tops should be smooth, washable, at least thirty inches wide, and whatever length is desirable—forty-eight to sixty inches. However, it must be remembered that too long a table is hard to move about and does not fit into floor plans easily.

There are small tables, eighteen by forty-eight inches, which are practical and may be used in various ways. They may be used singly when planned for the use of one or two children, or two tables may be placed together when needed by a group of five or six children.

Sturdy tables with folding legs may be desirable where play space is needed. These may be set up only when they are to be in special use. However, the construction must be strong or the legs will soon become insecure.

In small rooms or crowded situations, where there is not room enough both for tables and for space to play, the tables should be eliminated; and the children can do their work on the floor or use their chair seats for tables as they sit on the floor.

If there is space it is desirable to have a small table for an interest center where the children may put their special treasures they have brought or where things of interest pertaining to the unit may be placed.

There should be a small tea table, perhaps eighteen by twenty-four inches or twenty by twenty inches, for use in the housekeeping corner.

Beauty Center Table

In every Kindergarten room there should be a small low table which will be used in the front of the room as a beauty center (or worship center as it is called in the departments for older children). On this should be placed a simple attractive cover, a Bible, an offering container, and a vase of flowers. Often the picture for the day, mounted attractively, will be placed here also.

Secretary's Table or Desk

The secretary must have a table or desk. If she has space in the large cabinet to put away the things she uses each Sunday, a table is more usable and seems to fit into the regular Kindergarten furnishings better. But if this space is not available in the cabinet, she should have a small, light-weight, flat-topped desk with drawers for holding supplies. In some churches the secretary's desk or table is placed in the hall just outside the Kindergarten room door.

Piano

A piano kept in tune and handled by the right pianist is a big help to the Kindergarten Department. But it is not a necessity, and more worth-while work may be done with no instrument than with a poor one or with a pianist who does not work in perfect harmony with the experiences of the children. A small piano is preferable. It is in keeping with the childlike furnishings of the room. An organ should never be used with young children as a substitute for a piano.

Play Center Furnishings

Since young children learn best through doing, things for them to do must be provided. These things must include materials for play because it is through play that a little child really learns to live. Toys that encourage co-operative play, creative expression, and dramatization of everyday experiences help the child to grow in a Christian way. These toys should be grouped in "centers" according to their use.

Building Center

Large wooden blocks afford the children much creative activity. Those called unit blocks are best, since they are made in corresponding sizes ($5\frac{1}{2}$ x $2\frac{3}{4}$ x $2\frac{3}{4}$ and multiples thereof) which will fit together. They can be purchased from educational supply houses or may be made from lightweight lumber and carefully sanded. If the blocks are to be made locally, a second choice in size would be two by four inch lumber, cut into two, four, eight, and sixteen inch lengths.

Large hollow blocks are fine if they can be afforded and if there is space to use and store them. Oftentimes such blocks on a smaller scale can be made from wooden boxes, such as chalk boxes, cigar boxes, or cheese boxes. These should be sandpapered and painted after the lids have been securely nailed on.

There must be a place where the blocks may be kept. Many churches provide low shelves where the blocks are to be stacked, but stacking blocks in orderly rows is sometimes hard and tiresome for young children. A large sturdy box on ball-bearing casters is a good storage place for blocks. This can be moved around as needed.

For use along with the blocks there should be strong wooden trucks large enough to haul the blocks, also smaller cars, boats, and trains that may be pulled by the children, and either rubber or wooden people and farm animals. All of these stimulate creative play and should be kept on shelves near the blocks if possible.

Housekeeping Center

Medium-sized dolls made of rubber or composition, unbreakable and washable, are the best choice for this center. They should have washable clothes which can be removed easily by the children. (Dresses that open all the way down the back and close with large snaps seem to be the most popular.) Blankets are always in demand.

There should be a doll bed sturdy enough for a child to sit on, and bedclothes for it, of course. There should be a tea table and unbreakable dishes and cooking utensils. Also there might be included a toy telephone, iron and ironing board, broom, mop and dustpan, and a doll carriage if space permits. A simple play stove and sink add to the pleasure of playing and working in the housekeeping center. These two can easily be made from apple crates. Two crates fastened together in such a way as to hold a refrigerator vegetable pan between them makes a good sink. Shelves can be placed inside the crates where dishes and cooking utensils can be placed. One crate with a hinged door fastened to the front for an oven makes a stove, especially if round burners are painted on the top and dresser drawer knobs are screwed into the top front for handles to turn on the burners. Of course this furniture should be sanded and enameled.

Picture Book Center

Children enjoy a special place where they may look at picture books. A low table or low shelf on which the books are placed and chairs set invitingly around make an acceptable spot for this activity.

Other Toys

Other things may be added to the equipment such as suitable wooden inlay puzzles, toy town peg sets, View-Masters, etc. No mechanical toys of any kind should ever be used in the Kindergarten. Only those things which encourage creative or co-operative play or which broaden the child's knowledge and his liking for the beautiful, and at the same time are within his ability to use and understand, should find their place in the Kindergarten.

Accessories

There are certain furnishings which, from a utilitarian standpoint, may not seem necessary, but which are a real contribution to the teaching values of a room. They are part of the atmosphere. Among the accessories of a room we think of pictures, rugs, draperies, stands or receptacles for growing plants, and vases. We also think of the treasures that teachers and children bring to share with each other.

Pictures

A room without pictures is bare indeed, and there should be a few well-chosen permanent pictures on the walls. In choosing these it is well to remember that children do not understand abstract things or symbolism. For instance, the beautiful, well-known picture of *Jesus, the Good Shepherd* is not a good choice for Kindergarten. To these children Jesus was a carpenter, not a shepherd, and they cannot understand the meaning of people being lost sheep.

The following is a list of some suggested pictures from which a few may be chosen, according to the size of the room and the availability of wall space.

Christ Blessing Little Children, Plockhorst
Jesus and the Children, Elsie Anna Wood
Jesus, the Children's Friend, Sallman
Christ with Children, Bella Vichon
Sistine Madonna, Raphael (detail only)
Birth of Jesus, Elsie Anna Wood
Any of the pictures of Jesus as a baby or boy, Elsie Anna Wood

One chosen from among the first four listed would be a good choice for a picture to be hung over the beauty or worship center.

In hanging a picture we should remember that it is being hung for the children and not for adults, and so should be low enough for them to enjoy.

Rug

A rug makes a happy gathering place for children. It adds also to the attractiveness of a Kindergarten room, if the color scheme is carefully chosen.

Curtains or Draperies

Curtains or draperies give a softening effect and add to the homelikeness of the room. Sheer cotton, cretonne, glazed chintz, are some of the materials which may be used, but always the colors should harmonize with the rest of the room and any figures on the material should not be too large or of too vivid a color. The curtains should be pushed to the sides of the window so as to let the light in.

Venetian blinds are very nice and regulate the light well, although they are expensive. If these blinds are used, a valance at the top is sometimes more effective than draperies at the sides.

Other Accessories

A growing plant, a colorful vase, treasures which the children or teachers may bring, all lend atmosphere and make the room a more desirable place in which to live.

The Teacher's Task

Some few Kindergarten teachers have a part in planning new church school rooms for the activities of little children. This group has a big responsibility—the responsibility of putting ideals into brick and mortar. The Boards of the different denominations are always ready to send recommendations and suggestions to committees writing for help along these lines.

Other Kindergarten teachers may not have the opportunity of helping to plan a part of a new building, but they do have the responsibility of giving to the children the best church school environment within their power to give.

Any room can be thoroughly cleaned. Since there is not a vast amount of training needed in order to handle a paintbrush, it is possible with a few cans of well-chosen paint to make a room more beautiful and harmonious. New curtains or draperies may be added to the windows. Perhaps the furniture could be rearranged to better advantage. If there are no shelves and the budget does not permit any, orange or lemon crates or apple boxes can be fixed up attractively into shelves. A teacher with a little imagination and an eye for beauty and some help from others can make the room a beautiful place where the children will enjoy coming to work and play and worship.

For Assignment and Discussion

1. The Kindergarten children in a certain church school have been meeting with the Primary children because there is only one piano for the use of both groups. Which is more important, the piano or

the separate room? If the two groups should decide to separate, which should have the piano?

2. Draw a plan of your Kindergarten room, indicating exposures, openings, and placement of furniture. What changes can you make to render it a better place for the children to meet?

3. Suppose you were to teach the Kindergarten children in a rural section and had been given the kitchen of the church as the only available room. What suggestions would you make for fixing and equipping the room?

4. Suggest possible equipment for a corner in the main room of a small church.

Helpful Books and Pamphlets

Equipment and Arrangement for Children's Groups in the Church, Kramer

Portfolio for Kindergarten Teachers and *Portfolio on Materials for Work and Play*, Association for Childhood Education, Washington, D. C.

Guiding the Young Child, Appendix III, edited by Heffernan

Living in the Kindergarten, Chapter XVI, Wills and Stegeman

Denominational leaflets and pamphlets

CHAPTER VI

Conversation

An Experience Which Aids the Religious Growth of Children

Whenever two or more people get together they start talking. Shut your eyes for a minute and quietly visualize the buzz of the various conversations that are going on in the world and their possible results. Many ideas are interchanged, much information given, planning done, and so on. Young children, too, can learn through listening to and talking with others, and this is an activity which will be a part of all other activities and which will aid in the religious growth of these children.

Values of Group Conversation in Kindergarten

1. Each contributor has a sense of satisfaction and a certain amount of self-respect.

When a teacher listens courteously and is really interested as Ned announces, "Our cat has three new kittens," the little boy feels very comfortable. When she asks questions about the kittens and guides the whole group into a happy discussion which finally leads the children to talk intimately to God about their pets, Ned feels that he has made a real contribution, and so there is present a sense of satisfaction and a certain amount of wholesome self-respect. Little children are not vastly different from adults in their desire for self-expression.

2. Tactful conversation often helps to put a timid child at ease.

Was there ever a time when, in a group of strangers whose interests you did not know, you were conscious of being painfully silent? Perhaps in your need someone next to you called your attention to the lovely vase of flowers on the table and asked, "Do you know the name of those flowers?" You *did* know the name. In fact, it would have been hard indeed for anyone to name a flower with which you were not familiar. From that time on you were at your ease. You could talk more intelligently of flowers than of anything else, and so you answered questions and told of certain interesting experiences which you had had. You forgot yourself, and you no longer felt timid.

In the same way a timid little child often is made to feel at ease if he is tactfully encouraged to talk about the thing in which he is interested. Perhaps he has on new shoes and you will speak to him of those. Sitting down beside him with a picture book may be the means of helping him talk to you and gain confidence in himself. Speaking of some of the play equipment or showing it to him and talking about it may make him feel more at ease. Conversing with him about any such things as these may help him to get his mind off himself and to forget his shyness.

3. *Conversation develops self-control and courtesy.*

Children soon learn, or may soon learn, that all should not talk at once. It requires a decided degree of self-control for a young child to wait his turn and not interrupt when others are speaking. Through guidance in conversation a child may gradually develop this self-control and courtesy which, after all, is a much-desired species of unselfishness, not always attained by adults.

4. *Conversation increases the vocabulary.*

We begin to learn new words by hearing someone else use them or by reading, but we do not make them our own until we have used them ourselves. Through conversation a child becomes acquainted with new words, and soon they become a part of his everyday intercourse. Think of some of the significant words a child may learn through conversation in the church school, such as, talking to God, share, good gifts, guests, minister, the friendly dark, the happy daytime, God's care through mothers and fathers or other loving helpers.

5. Conversation helps a teacher to know the real interests, needs, and capacities of the children.

The teacher who engages in a monologue instead of conversation never knows the real interests, needs, and capacities of the children. Oh, that teachers might talk less and listen more! It is so much easier for an untrained teacher to "tell things" to a group than to lead the children to ask questions or share knowledge. For this reason she falls into the habit of singing songs, telling stories, or saying verses, with a vague feeling, it is true, that at times the children are not particularly interested. In fact, they do not seem really to need the material she is using. She often has a distinct impression that she has overestimated the mental capacity of some members of her group; and at other times she feels that she has underestimated their capacity. This impression, however, is a bit vague. It is borne in on her by a blank expression on most of the faces, or by what in an older person would be called a bored expression, accompanied by restlessness. If only she would converse with the children instead of doing all the talking herself, she would find herself teaching children instead of materials or lessons.

The following are comments made by some of the children in a weekday Kindergarten while each was working on a paper-doll family, and during later conversation about the family groups. The "reporter" has included explanations which throw a great deal of light upon the children's comments.

Lorena in choosing and pasting her family had placed father and mother and a girl of about twelve whom she called Mary Ann her sister, and who she said helped mother lots and went to Memorial (Junior High). I questioned it because I thought she was an only child, but she told me so many things this sister did about the home that I decided I was wrong. Then she placed a little girl of about five years of age on the paper and I wrote her name under the picture. Later as they were talking and pointing out their families, Lorena named father and mother, then said the five-year-old was her little sister and she herself was Mary Ann (the twelve-year-old). Upon closer questioning she admitted that she had always wanted to be named Mary Ann and that she wanted to be big enough to help her mother and to go to Memorial. (Her mother has been sick for more than a year and evidently has not wanted to be bothered by letting the child help her.) I commended her for wanting to help and tried to suggest ways she could help now, with the children of course aiding the conversation.

Billy V., to my surprise, placed only himself and father and mother on his paper (which was right). At Christmas he had insisted that he had a baby sister, told us her name, how he helped mother bathe and dress her, what she was fed, and so forth, and that he must make her a Christmas present or she might cry. He had talked about her so much that I had expected him to put her with his family. In talking about it he said, looking at the baby pictures longingly, "I wish I could put Betty Ann on, but she isn't really our family."

Myrna: "I can't put my daddy on, 'cause he's in heaven, but maybe I could cut him out anyway." (She didn't, however.)

Ronald (whose father and mother are separated): "I'm putting my daddy right here by my mother, and then I'll have to put Mrs. Fernandez on, 'cause she looks after me while Mother's at the office."

Billy C. has a mother and little sister, but lives with them in the home of Mr. and Mrs. Peters who have three girls, so he insisted on putting the Peters family on the back of his paper.

Martha lives with her father and mother in the home of her grandmother, in which home there also live three grown sisters and a grown brother of her father's. She decided to do the same as Billy, and put her own family on one side and the others on the back, but she had quite a time deciding on which side to put her grandmother, since her grandmother takes care of her while her mother teaches. Also one of the aunts was married two weeks ago, and Martha hesitated about including her, but finally decided not to, saying, "Of course I guess she's still a part of the family, but she has a man now to look after her, so I won't have to worry about her any more."

Johnny: "I didn't put my grandmother on because I couldn't find one that looked like her, but I left a place for her."

Martha: "I can't find one that looks like my grandmother, either, so I'll just put a young one on. Anyway, she isn't very old, but she is fatter than this picture."

Johnny (after discussion of pictures): "Why don't you tell us a story about families now?" I proceeded to do this immediately.

6. *Conversation presents an opportunity for giving information at an appropriate time.*

How much better it is to tell the story, "David Playing for the King," after conversation about happiness and doing things to make other people happy than to tell it as a mere story!

The story of the guestroom built for Elisha will have more significance for the children if it is told after a conversation about the kind of houses in which many people of those days lived—about the flat roofs and the outside steps.

Often songs are much more appropriate as a part of conversation than when introduced merely as songs. An illustration of this is found in the record of conversation given on page 82 when the song, "Work for All," was introduced and used many times throughout the discussion. Bible stories, pictures, handwork activities, and make-believe play are all better understood when introduced by conversation.

7. *Conversation is a means of planning together.*

Very often the teacher and children need to plan together for some activity for which they are preparing, and conversation is a very important part of this planning.

One of the girls in a certain Kindergarten group had been quite sick in the hospital and every Sunday the children asked about her. The teacher felt this interest could be guided into action—doing something for the sick friend. So they talked about it and all of the children were eager to help. They gave many suggestions, some of which were not practicable, but finally decided to make her some picture scrapbooks and a long picture letter—each child drawing a picture which would be pasted with all the others on a roll of shelf paper, to be unrolled as she wanted to look at them. They discussed what kind of pictures would be good for the scrapbooks and also what they should draw that would hold her interest. Then they went to work eagerly and everyone helped in the activity which had been carefully planned as they talked together.

During a unit about the church, a teacher wanted to take the children through the sanctuary. So they gathered together to plan for the trip. They discussed how they would walk, how they would talk, what they would look for; and

the trip was made a meaningful and reverent experience because of the conversation which took place first as they
planned together.

*8. Conversation gives an opportunity for correcting wrong
impressions.*

If space permitted, incident after incident could be cited
to show that young children—even children under the guidance of thoughtful parents and teachers—often receive
wrong impressions. These impressions are most often re-
vealed through conversation. The teacher will revise and
retell a certain story, will make an explanation of certain
words in a song, or will otherwise tactfully correct wrong
conceptions on the part of certain ones in her group.

*9. Conversation, to some extent, is a means of evaluating
past teaching and activities.*

The discussion in the last paragraph bears on the question
of the evaluation of past teaching, but only treats one side
of the subject—and that the negative side. It is helpful to
learn of mistakes in order that they may be corrected, but
it is equally helpful and more encouraging to learn of successes. Teaching is a joy when Franklin confides that he is
not afraid of the dark any more; when John lets you know
that he stopped while riding on his tricycle to say, "Thank
You," to God; when Lena says, "I just love Jesus. He is
so kind."

Conversation is not, it is true, an absolutely accurate means
of evaluating past teaching, for children at times claim un-
deserved credit for virtues and imagine themselves better
than they are, but certainly their conversation does help us
to evaluate our teaching.

Often experiences and activities just completed need to be
evaluated by the children, and talking it over is the only way
to do this. If, during a unit on the home, the children were
led to want to help in their homes and had planned to do
some definite helping during the week, then the following
Sunday there certainly should be a time for reporting and
talking over what was done.

During a unit on "Beautiful Things God Has Made," the children were invited to see a lovely garden. Everything went well until they saw a squirrel and several started chasing him, tramping over some of the flowers. When they returned to the church the group were gathered together to talk things over and the children made some rules of conduct to be followed on future excursions. Incidentally, two of the offenders asked the teacher if she would write a letter to the owner of the garden asking what they could do to "fix the garden back right," since the discussion had not yielded any suggestions of actual things to do other than to apologize and promise better behavior in the future!

Rules for Guiding Conversation in the Kindergarten

While there can be no ironclad rules for conversation in a church school Kindergarten, the following suggestions might be termed "elastic" rules for guiding the conversation.

1. Have in mind a definite goal to be reached, or a purpose to be accomplished.

It is easy to be "side-tracked," as it were, and to talk about trivial things or to pursue in a purposeless manner subjects that might be significant if developed.

It is true that courtesy and good teaching recognize the fact that the best conversational procedure is not always a direct route from Starting Point to Goal, or objective, but

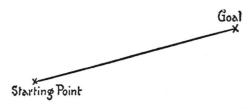

is so controlled that each departure is utilized, if possible, and made a contributing factor.

The following is a stenographic report of conversational teaching with one group of Kindergarten children. It shows how the teacher tried to stick to her purpose and how some of the responses of the children could have sidetracked her.

CARING FOR GROWING THINGS

Leader's Purpose: To help the children realize that it is God's plan for people to work with Him in caring for growing things.

When the children first arrived, they had several experiences of planting. One group planted seeds in a window box; another transplanted some plants into coffee cans; and a third placed ivy in jars of water and anchored it with marbles. They brought all these things to show when the whole group was gathered together and some from each small group explained what had been done. Then this conversation followed.

Teacher: All of you worked to help plant things this morning. (Singing without any special introduction)

> "There is work that all may do,
>   Helping in God's world;
> Work for me and work for you,
>   Helping in God's world."

Have any of you ever helped plant a garden outdoors?

Chorus: I have! I have!

Johnny: Daddy and me made a *big* garden.

Tommy: My daddy can make a bigger garden than your daddy. He made one this big. (And he walked around to show how big.)

Teacher: Johnny, what did Daddy and you plant in your garden?

Johnny: I don't know.

Teacher: Was it something to eat or was it flowers?

Tommy (interrupting): I can tell you what I planted.

Teacher: In just a minute, Tommy. Johnny is answering my question now.

Johnny: I don't know what it was, 'cause it never came up.

Tommy (laughing boisterously): You must not know how to plant things.

Teacher: Sometimes seeds don't grow. They might not have been good seeds with life in them, or there may have been something wrong with the ground. Tommy, what did you plant?

Tommy: We planted everything—radishes and beans and—and—and—.

Mary: I thought he said he planted everything.

Teacher: Who else has planted a garden?

Sara: I have a flower garden. Daddy dug it up for me, but I planted it.

Teacher: You and Daddy both worked, didn't you? (Starts singing) "There is work that all may do." (Two children join her in the refrain, "Helping in God's world.") If we were to plant a garden what would be the first thing to do?

Chorus: Dig it—hoe it—no, rake it.

Teacher: Let's play like we are digging up a garden. How would we do it?

Jim: Take your shovel and dig up the dirt.

(All do it in pantomime.)

Teacher: I like to sing while I work. (Starts singing: "There is work that all may do"—several join with her.)

Teacher: What do we do next?

Several: Chop it. No, rake it. Let's hoe it.

Mary: We have to rake it smooth. My mother rakes her garden.

Teacher: Let's rake our gardens.

Sara: We ought to sing.

(All sing "There is work that all may do" as they rake.)

Teacher: Now, what should we do?

Jim: Plant the seeds. But you better make a line in the dirt first so you can get it straight. That's what my dad does.

(They all pantomime planting the seeds and follow the teacher's action of covering up the seeds.)

Teacher: Now what do we do?

Sara: Go play.

Teacher: But I think maybe we should do something first to help those seeds.

Mary: Let's water them. (They play watering.)

Tommy (shouting): I've got a hose. I'm going to water you! (And he points his finger at some of the other children.)

Teacher (immediately starting to sing): "There is work that all may do." (Most of the others join her in singing instead of following Tommy's lead.)

Teacher: Sometimes we don't need to water our gardens. What often waters them for us?

Chorus: The rain. The rain.

Sara: The rain and the sun both make them grow.

Ted: The sun makes us grow, too.

Alice: The sun doesn't make me grow—it makes me red.

Teacher: Maybe that is because you stayed out in the sunshine too long at the beach. (Alice had just returned from a stay at the beach.)

(The teacher realized her mistake as soon as she said the word "beach," for several immediately wanted to tell about the beach. She acknowledged their contributions with a nod of the head, then continued.)

Teacher: Does anything grow on the beach?

Tommy: Seaweed.

Alice: There were some flowers growing around the house where we stayed.

Teacher: That would be pretty. What helped those flowers to grow?

Alice: The sunshine and the rain.

Teacher: Who planned for the sunshine and rain to help those flowers to grow?

Chorus: God.

Teacher (starting a story): Once a mother wanted a garden. (Continued with a story about two children helping their mother plant a garden. At the conclusion of the story she showed a large picture of the mother and two children working in a garden.)

Teacher: Everyone in the picture is working. What is the mother doing?

Children: Hoeing.

Teacher (to child who has taken no part in the conversation so far): Fred, what is the girl doing?

Fred: She must be pulling weeds.

Teacher (to another child who has taken no part so far): Carol, what is the boy doing?

Carol: He's carrying water.

Teacher: All of them are working—helping in God's world. Let's sing our song and you play like you are the boy or the girl helping in the garden.

(All take part in the singing and pantomiming.)

Teacher: Let's sit down and think a minute. God has planned for people to work with Him in caring for growing things. I am going to tell some things about gardens and you tell me whether it is what people do or what God plans for.

Teacher: Who planned for the ground for things to grow in?

Children: God.

Teacher: Who digs up the ground?

Children: People.

Teacher: Who plants the seeds?

Children: People. (One child said, "God," then quickly changed.)

Teacher: Who planned for seeds to have life in them and grow?

Children: God.

Teacher: Who waters the garden with watering cans or the hose?
Children: People.
Teacher: Who planned the water for gardens?
Children: God.
Teacher: Who planned for sunshine to make the plants grow?
Children: God.
Teacher: Who picks the vegetables or fruit after they have grown?
Children: People.
Teacher: God has a part and people have a part in caring for growing things. That is one way we can help God—by helping to care for growing things. There is a verse in the Bible which says (reading from the Bible I Corinthians 3:9), "We are fellow-workers with God." That means—we are workers together with God.

Tommy: I can say that. It's easy. "We are workers together with God."

Teacher: Let's all say it. (All do.) Our song says it in different words. Let's sing it. (All sing—"There is work that all may do," etc.)

Teacher: I am glad God lets us help in His world. I would like to talk to Him about it. (Bowing her head and praying.) Dear God, we're glad you let us help take care of growing things. Help us to remember to do our part. Amen.

2. Courteously ignore topics which in your judgment should not be developed.

Not all topics are equally fruitful, nor are all topics of equal religious significance. It is a bit painful, at times, to witness the efforts of certain conscientious modern teachers who have had just enough training to find themselves endeavoring to turn into a religious channel every remark made by a child. The child who saw "a dead horse on the side of the road" need not be frowned upon, but the topic should be ignored so far as any group development is concerned. It sometimes happens that something which has made an unpleasant impression on a child should be told to someone as a relief. In this case the teacher might say, "Go over and tell it to Mrs. . . . ." (one of the assistants, who should take the child to one side).

Certain home happenings, the discussion of which would be embarrassing to the "grown-ups" concerned, should be ignored. A little child will often innocently divulge the most private concerns of his family, if allowed to do so. The teacher with refined instincts will sense this and tactfully guide the conversation into safer channels.

3. Do not cut off abruptly a child who desires to contribute.

It is true that not every remark contributed by a child can or should be developed, but there is a fineness of feeling— a sympathy—on the part of the true teacher that will accept these would-be contributions with a kindness and courtesy that warms the heart of a timid child and lets no child feel uncomfortable.

4. Do not encourage one child or a few children to do all of the talking.

It is easy to use John's contributions. He likes to talk, has a keen mind, and expresses himself in such a way that the whole teaching process seems to move rapidly. We find ourselves helping John to develop, but forgetting to provide opportunities for quiet little Mildred who needs help more. It is a good plan, now and then, to check ourselves to see whether or not all the children in our group are being developed.

5. Word your questions clearly, one at a time, and avoid all ambiguous questions.

Do not say, "Can you think of a boy who helped and a girl who took care of her brother?"

The following are examples of questions which may lead children to think:

"Which child should you like to have been?" (Looking at Plockhorst's picture, "Christ Blessing Little Children.")

"Can you tell me the name of this flower?" (Holding a flower for the children to touch and see.)

"What can a child do to help Mother?" (Developing a child's part in making home a happy place.)

"How can a child help God to take care of His flowers?" (After an appreciation of growing things, as a first approach to working with God.)

6. Introduce easy and fruitful topics of conversation.

Four- and five-year-old children spend most of their time in their homes. The topics which will be of most interest to them are those that have to do with the everyday home surroundings or happenings. Their toys and pets, as well as playmates and other people who touch the home life, are fruitful topics.

7. Wait patiently for responses, but do not let the conversation drag.

We often make the mistake of asking questions that require either too much thought, or needed information, before they can be answered.

It is not easy to give to an untrained teacher advice about how long to wait for an answer to a question. In most cases there should be a short pause only. Some of us wait too long, not sensing the fact that we have made a mistake in assuming on the part of the children the interest, knowledge, and mental capacity needed for an answer. The result is a restlessness in the group which might have been avoided.

8. Whenever possible, allow and encourage children to give information.

What has just been said does not contradict the practice of encouraging children to give as much information as possible. It is a fairly safe rule not to tell children something that they can find out for themselves, and it is often better to let a child share his information with the group than for the teacher to do so. There will be many times when it will be necessary for the teacher to share her knowledge and experience. She must sense these times, but wisely refrain from monopolizing.

When to Engage in Conversation

As has surely been made clear in all this discussion, there is no set time in the Kindergarten session for conversation. It should permeate the whole procedure. It may come before or after a new song, or an old one for that matter; it may come as the children look at a picture or examine a bird's nest; it may come as a preface to a prayer, or while the teacher turns the pages of the Bible to find a favorite verse; it may prepare for a story or vitalize dramatization; it may lend zest and meaning to handwork activity, or give purpose to games.

Group conversation is valuable, but sometimes the most profitable conversation takes place when a leader or an assistant is conversing with one child only, engaged in work or play activities.

One of the times that is apt to prove most fruitful in conversational responses is ignored by teachers who do not realize that the session begins when the first child arrives. These early moments when a teacher may talk with one child as he works or plays often reveal characteristics and ideas that are undiscovered in group conversation.

It must be remembered that conversation is for the development of the individuals rather than of ideas. The whole program is for the children. Their opinions and questions are to be considered, and they should be given frequent opportunities for voicing questions and sharing experiences. In this way they may be helped to grow religiously.

For Assignment and Discussion

1. Read carefully the stenographic report of conversation given in this chapter under "Conversational Rules," and note the times when the responses of a child might have diverted the conversation into channels which had no bearing on the purpose the leader had in mind.

2. Visit a Kindergarten or check your own Kindergarten session and note, as accurately as you can, all the conversations that took place. Might they have been handled in a better way?

Helpful Books

Living in the Kindergarten, Chapter IX, Wills and Stegeman
Guiding the Young Child, Chapter VIII, edited by Heffernan.
Education in the Kindergarten, Chapter XVII, Foster and Headley, second edition.

CHAPTER VII

Worship

An Experience Which Aids the Religious Growth of Children

Worship is the communion of a child with God the Father. There can be no higher purpose of religious education than that of leading children into a vital relationship with God—of making Him so real that children will instinctively turn to Him in their joys and perplexities, at home, at church school, and day school—in work and play.

Times for Worship

In the Kindergarten there is no set time for worship as there may be with older groups. Any moment, even in the midst of some activity, when the children feel the nearness of God or gratitude to Him, will be the time to express their thoughts to Him with the teacher's guidance. Certain materials such as Bible verses, stories, or incidents, short poems, songs, pictures, or nature materials may help children to worship, and often the Kindergarten teacher plans to use these things to try to help bring God near. But even though after much thought she may have a certain spot for worship written down in her plans, still she cannot be sure that that time will be best. The children will have to be in the right mood or it will have no meaning. Therefore, the teacher will have to be able to sense the moment when the children may feel near to God and want to talk to Him.

In a unit about the church, a teacher had very carefully planned her entire procedure. She wanted to guide the children to an appreciation of the church and an enjoyment of being in church. She hoped to encourage some of the children to build a block church, then to gather the others around to see it and talk about it. Next all were to go to the "big church" to look at the beautiful windows, the pulpit, the organ, the pews, and all the other things there. After they came back to their own room they would discuss what they saw, and after some suitable songs and using the Bible verse, "I was glad when they said to me, 'Let us go to the house of the Lord,'" she hoped to be able to lead the children to a moment of worship and of thanking God for the church.

But things did not go as she had planned. An adult class had a committee meeting in the sanctuary at the time she wanted to take the children there. She learned of the meeting just before they were ready to go, so she went ahead with the songs and Bible verse in the Kindergarten room, but she did not voice the prayer as planned, for the children were restless and noisy. By the time she could take them to the sanctuary she was concerned over how they might act there. But as they entered the side door of the church, one of the children noticed the sunshine streaming through the large stained-glass window at the back. It was beautiful, and he pointed to it and said softly, "Look!" Everyone did look and not a word was spoken for a few minutes. The teacher could sense the feeling among the children and she started saying softly, "I was glad when they said to me—" and the boys and girls all joined her, saying it very softly, too. Then she prayed very simply, "Thank you, God, for our church." She was sure that the children had joined with her in the thought of the prayer and that all had a feeling of worship.

That was spontaneous worship. The teacher had planned that the prayer would come at a different time in the procedure, but she was quick to grasp a moment when it reflected the mood of the children.

Praying and "Saying Prayers"

When Jesus lived on the earth, His disciples, spiritually hungry, begged, "Lord, teach us to pray."

Throughout the ages hungry hearts have felt the need of fuller communion with God, and have cried out, "Lord, teach us to pray!"

When this prayer has been prayed sincerely by a teacher of Kindergarten children, her next request should be, "Lord, teach me how to teach these children to pray."

"Teaching young children to pray" does not mean "teaching young children to say prayers." It means leading these children into the very closest communion with God, teaching them to speak to Him often in their joys or sorrows, in their playtime or quiet rest times, at stated times or at any time.

The Elements of Prayer

As we think of how we can teach children to pray, it may help if we consider the elements of an adult's prayer and see if these same elements may be found in the prayers of young children.

Adoration

Translated into a child's vocabulary, adoration means, "I love you, God."

The wise teacher or parent will not demand the words before the desire to express them is aroused. The little child loves most those who do most for him—provided the service rendered is on his own plane of appreciation. For example, his mother is loved because she tells stories to him, or gives him his food, or plays with him, or stays close by when he is frightened. He seems to love God in the same way.

First of all comes the realization that God has planned for the beautiful things about him which give him pleasure.

The little child asking his first questions, on seeing the moon, said, "What's that?"

"We call it 'the moon,'" was the answer.

"Who made it?" asked the child.

"God made the moon," was the mother's answer.

"Pretty moon, pretty God," came from the little boy's lips, as he looked wonderingly up into the night sky.

And so his first communion with God held the element of adoration.

There are frequent opportunities in the church school for the expression of adoration. In the midst of activities which induce worship there are many times when children will gladly pause and say, either in words or in the expression of their faces, "I love You, God."

Thanksgiving

Very soon the expression of a sincere love for God and appreciation of His gifts is possible. "Thank You, God," comes very naturally into children's hearts and finds expression on children's lips, if wise parents and teachers take the time to lead them to an understanding of God's part in providing for their needs.

It is rather important to show to them as much of God's method of doing this as they are capable of understanding. They may be allowed to stand in wonder before the sunset or the evening stars, before an opening flower or a tree, while you whisper, "God our Father planned that for us." But, "God our loving Father gave your nice breakfast to you," needs more explanation. Before this statement should come the story of the growing and care of food-producing plants —of God's gift of rain and sunshine, and of the work shared by those who sow the seed, care for the plants, and gather the crop. When the little child truly understands, his thanksgiving is very real—perhaps most real because his very egoism makes him feel that the gifts were made just for him.

Church school teachers need to be careful in safeguarding the prayers of thanksgiving. It is so easy to say to the children, "What do you want to thank God our Father for today?" and to receive practically the same answer each Sunday. Do not use this method so often that it will become fixed. Frequently use special reasons for thanksgiving.

Supplication

Supplication is not, perhaps, one of the first elements of a child's prayer, although he learns very soon to say "God

bless Mother," and "God bless Daddy," and "God bless me."
Sometimes "and make me a good boy" is added. It is not easy
to make these phrases really meaningful, but a beginning
can be made.

The kind of supplication that is the most difficult to safe-
guard is the prayer for material things. The faith of a young
man was weakened because when he was a child and prayed
for material gifts his parents always managed, if possible, to
see that the gifts came to him. Later on he came to realize
what had been done and to realize that when he did not pray
audibly his prayers for material gifts were not always answered in the affirmative. He lived for many years before
realizing that a wise God often says "No" instead of "Yes."
It is much more wholesome for a child to understand that
God is saying "No" than to feel that his prayer is not
answered.

Sometimes children get the idea that God is merely a sort
of glorified Santa Claus. This was evidenced in a recent report by a relative of two very little children who decided
one day that they would "play being God." The older one
climbed to the top of the piano and threw toys to the
younger, who stood with hands posed in a supplicating attitude. After a few minutes the little one took her turn at
"being God," and the positions were reversed.

This incident startles us, it is true, but it calls us to task
for some of our past methods of teaching children to pray.
The wise parent and teacher will put the emphasis on spiritual
rather than on material gifts.

As will be seen in the following report, one of our church
school teachers most wisely helped to give a true and sane
foundation for the prayers of supplication of a little boy.

On the Sunday following the story of "David, the Shepherd Boy,"
the teacher and the group were talking of how God helped David.
This naturally led to the discussion of "God is my helper."
Y. W. said, "Miss Jean, will God help me to hop?"
Miss Jean replied, "I am sure he will, if you try."
Several days later the children older than Y.W. were playing hop-
scotch on the sidewalk in front of his house. Y. W. watched them
hop and tried to hop but he could not. That night when he went to

bed he prayed, "Dear God, help me to hop like Mary and John" (his older brother and sister).

Several days after this the children were playing again. Y. W. watched them. He tried and tried and finally caught on to the idea of hopping. On he hopped up and down, unconscious of anyone looking at him. His mother heard him at the top of his voice say, "Thank You, God. Thank You." Then he ran as fast as he could to the porch where his mother was seated, his face beaming with joy. "Mother, Miss Jean said He would help me if I tried, and He did," he exclaimed.[1]

Submission

Submission on the part of a child is a willingness to do God's way because it is pleasing to God the Father, and a willingness to accept the gifts provided, even though something else was desired.

This element rarely sincerely creeps into the prayers of children. It is an element, for that matter, that is often lacking in adult prayers. It can, however, have its beginning in children's prayers.

I know of a five-year-old who accepted a rainy day at home instead of enjoying a picnic with the statement, "I 'spose God knew the flowers needed water."

Confession

Confession of wrongdoing is an element which parents, rather than church school teachers, should feel responsible for developing.

It is not wise to lead a child to confess publicly to God his personal shortcomings, but in the intimate bedtime hour he may be led to pray truly, "I'm sorry, God, that I didn't let Buntie ride on my scooter. Help me to remember to share my toys."

This, however, should come after conversation about the day's happenings, and should be very sincere and not a repetition only of the mother's words.

Companionship

Communion with God means more than talking to Him. There is a sense of companionship that does not adequately

---

[1] Reported by a teacher.

express itself in adoration or thanksgiving, and that does not ask for anything. Even a child may feel this. Perhaps the easiest way to define this sense of companionship as felt by a child is to recall "An Extra Prayer."

> Sometimes I say an extra prayer,
>   Besides the one for which I kneel.
> I stand and look up at the stars,
>   And tell our Father how I feel.
>
> I do not ask for anything;
>   I just feel happy through and through:
> I let my heart give thanks and sing,
>   Till all the world seems good and true.
> —*Annie Willis McCullough.*[2]

Methods differ and vocabularies differ, but sincere communion between God and His older and younger children is much the same in its elements; and it may help if we remember this and hold to essentials in studying children's prayers.

Form Prayers

The question is often asked by parents and teachers, "Shall we teach our children forms of prayer?"

A form prayer holds certain values, but certainly contains dangerous elements as well.

A form prayer is valuable for the following reasons:

1. It teaches a certain vocabulary of prayer.
2. It may express a child's own thoughts as he could never express them unaided.
3. It sometimes increases the range of thought of the one who prays, reacting on his own experience.
4. It helps to socialize the group, when entered into by several persons, and so broadens and enriches the experiences of each member of the group.

All this sounds a bit technical in talking about a young child's approach to God. Perhaps illustrating these values will help.

1. Just as a child is taught, when forming his first sen-

---

[2] From *Songs for Little People*, Danielson and Conant, Copyrighted. Used by permission of Pilgrim Press, publishers.

tences, to say, "Thank you, Mother," or "Thank you, Daddy," he may be taught to say, "Thank You, God." We should be very careful, however, to know that he is really thankful before encouraging him to say the words. Thus the words will be a sincere expression of real feeling.

2. Someone has said, "As soon as we read or hear our own thoughts better expressed than we could express them, we realize at once that they are our own thoughts and that we are better and stronger for their adequate expression." [3]

Does not a child, when he hears a simple, beautiful prayer, worded on the plane of his understanding, often feel, even though he may never say so in words, "That's just what I wanted to say to God"?

3. The Kindergarten child's range of thought is increased by leading him to think of some of the definite objects of his thanksgiving. A form of prayer which helps to do this is:

"Thank You, Father, for the sky;
    For the sun and rain and snow;
Thank You for the stars at night;
    Thank You for the winds that blow.

"Thank You for the birds and trees;
    For the flowers that bloom so fair;
Thank You for the food we eat;
    Thank You for Your love and care." [4]

4. As prayers are earnestly prayed by a group of children, there is something in the group response and the appreciation of all the children which reacts on each child. This is what we mean by socializing the group and enriching the experience of each member.

A form prayer has a place in group worship, provided the emphasis is not put upon this kind of prayer, and provided the same form is not used too often.

Occasionally the children can have a responsive part in a form of prayer in which the leader enumerates the objects of thanksgiving and the children join with her in the simple

---

[3] Dr. Alphonso Smith in *What Literature Means to Me.*
[4] Myrtle Williamson, in *Worship and Conduct Songs.* Copyrighted, 1926, by Elizabeth McE. Shields.

phrase, "Thank You, God." This is called a litany. For example, perhaps the children have mentioned things for which they can thank God, and the teacher will use these suggestions something like this:

Teacher: For all we have to eat—apples and oranges and meat and bread—
Children: Thank You, God.
Teacher: For our clothes we wear—our dresses and suits and coats and shoes—
Children: Thank You, God.
Teacher: For our homes—our fathers and mothers and sisters and brothers—
Children: Thank You, God.
Teacher: For all our friends we play with and have such good times with—
Children: Thank You, God.

Or instead of the words, "Thank You, God," the refrain may be a Bible verse of praise, such as, "We give thanks to thee, O God." (Psalm 75:1a, R.S.V.)

Song prayers are, of course, forms. They hold a very dear place in the hearts of children, and many children as they sing them are truly praying. This is apt to be the case when the songs have been taught as prayers and when they are always so used.

One example of this type of song is:

> Thank You for the world so sweet,
> Thank You for the food we eat,
> Thank You for the birds that sing,
> Thank You, God, for everything.

(The music for this song is found on page 121.)

There are many songs which are not prayers but which help to bring children into an atmosphere of prayer. The prayer in this case may not be voiced, or it may take real form on the child's lips.

A group of Kindergarten children were taught the song which begins:

> I wake in the morning,
>   As soon as it's light;
> I thank our kind Father,
>   For watch care at night.

A few days after the song was introduced, Alston said: "You know that song about 'I wake in the morning'? Well, I waked up singing it this morning."

Who shall say that he did not really thank God our Father for His watch care?

The kind of prayer induced by a song will, in a few cases, be a form, but often it is a prayer not voiced, or a prayer worded spontaneously by the child.

There are, however, as has been stated, grave dangers in adhering too much to forms of prayer. There is the danger of using the same form too often. If this is done, there is no enrichment of experience. In this case the use of the prayer is of little more value than the turning of a "prayer wheel." It resolves into a mere use of words, and becomes mechanical. An example of the difficulty of breaking away from a form prayer was shown in a vacation school, at the close of a day when the children had had an unusually good time. Someone suggested thanking God for their good time. One of the children who had not sufficiently developed her prayer life immediately suggested the only prayer she knew which seemed to her suitable:

> "Thou art great, Thou art good,
> And we thank Thee for our food."

One of the more thoughtful children said, "But it isn't food, it's a good time. Let's say:

> " 'Thou art great, Thou art good,
> And we thank Thee for our good time.' "

And they did!

The following are suggested prayers which may be used by parents and teachers who feel the need of forms:

> We give our thanks to You, O God,
> For rest and food and play;
> For loving us and helping us
> At all times, night and day.

Dear God, to us You are so good,
We thank You for Your gift of food.[5]

Thank You, God, for _____ and _____,[*]
   And other things so good.
Thank You, God, for those who help
   To grow and cook our food.
(*Insert names of food on table, such as milk and bread.)

Spontaneous Prayers

The spontaneous prayer as used in the church school is the prayer which is voiced in the teacher's own words or in the child's own words at any time in the experience of the day. It is by far the most valuable prayer.

1. It may come after a song.

A joyous hush had come over a group of children at Christmastime when they had finished singing "Away in a Manger," and a little four-year-old said, "That song just makes me happy." It made everybody happy, and the simple, "Thank You, God, for sending little Jesus," was voiced by the teacher, but was really prayed by all the children.

2. It may come after a story.

A teacher told the story, "Jesus Loving Little Children," and there was so much joy and thankfulness in the faces of the children that a prayer just said itself—"We are so glad for Jesus, who loves us and all little children."

3. It may come when looking at a picture.

As the children are earnestly handling and discussing the picture, perhaps a child says, "I believe that they are saying 'Thank You!'" "I believe they are," says the teacher. "Perhaps, you would like to say 'Thank You,' too." The earnest voices then speak a real "Thank You."

4. It may come while enjoying some of God's creations.

One of the nearest roads from the heart of a child to God is through nature. It is easy for the church school teacher or

---

[5] This grace and the preceding prayer are by Dorothae G. Mallard.

parent to associate the song of the birds, the sunshine, the blooming of the flowers, the trees, the evening stars, with Him who created them.

Not all of these can be brought into the church school, although the resourceful teacher will see that her children are constantly in contact with, and reminded of, God's creations. Associations can be made that may carry over into the everyday experiences of the children.

A definite response was noted in one group when the teacher let each child smell the first narcissus that bloomed, singing over and over Van Dyke's beautiful words:

> "Every morning seems to say,
> 'There's something happy on the way
> And God sends love to you.'" [6]

The following interesting experience has been reported:

A four-year-old girl was in the garden one sunny spring day. After looking at the flowers for a while, she dropped on her knees beside a bed of jonquils and began to talk with great earnestness. An adult relative, noticing the child, stepped nearer and observed that she had her lips close to the cup of a large jonquil as she talked. When she rose and left the flower, the adult asked her why she was talking to that flower, and the child, looking quite amazed at the ignorance of an adult, said, "I was telephoning to God. Didn't you know that they are God's telephones?" [7]

"Nature rightly interpreted speaks of her Creator." The prayer life of a child may be greatly enriched when a true interpreter takes his hand.

5. It may come at odd times impossible to designate.

The children and teacher had been talking about things God had made and the teacher said, "I feel like going to the window where we may see some of these things, and speaking to God. All who feel the same way may go with me." As a number of the children followed, she asked, "What would you like to say?" One voice answered, "I love You, God," and other voices joined in.

[6] Used by permission of Charles Scribner's Sons.

[7] From a poem by Annie G. Freeman, *Children's Leader,* April, 1929. A true record of experience. Used by permission.

The teacher who is keen to watch for chances for spontaneous prayer may discover them in unexpected places— in song, creative work, and story, or in the midst of conversation, or play, or the solving of a puzzling problem. A real opportunity for spontaneous prayer often comes when the children are in the midst of a sharing project. They like to talk to God about their efforts for others. They can easily be led to think of themselves as working with God, and talking to Him about their joint work will be natural. Often the children themselves will find an opportunity and suggest prayer.

There is, however, even in spontaneous prayers, a danger of dragging them in, as it were, and making them so commonplace that they will lose their significance and beauty.

The most important thing to teach young children is not the joy of praying in the church school, but the joy of praying any time and anywhere. The leaders in a vacation school tried to emphasize this by the use of one of Jessie Eleanor Moore's stories, "Anytime, Anywhere." It was a joyous moment for the teachers when little John, on hearing the story the second time, seemed very appreciative as the hero stopped while riding on his kiddie car to say "Thank You" to God. He hardly interrupted the storyteller as he said, almost to himself: "That's just what I did yesterday on my tricycle."

The terms, "heavenly Father," or "our Father," should be avoided with Kindergarten children, as we cannot be sure that the children understand that God is the One so addressed. Many teachers feel that it is better to use only the word "God" at all times. But if other terms are used, the word "God" should always be used with them to be sure the children will not confuse "our Father" with their own fathers.

Also it is better if the prayer is always addressed to God instead of to Jesus, since children may become confused over this, too.

Prayer in the Home

It is in the home that a sense of the nearness of God can most truly be developed—in that intimate atmosphere where a mother or a father can associate everyday happenings with God the Father.

The form prayer should not have a large place here. It may occasionally be used to help to express a child's ideas, but it should never take the place of the effort which a child should make to express his own thoughts.

It is easy for parents to guide their young children into informal expression. Perhaps the reason it is not done oftener is that it takes more time and thought than the quickly said form prayer. The beautiful example of a child's spontaneous prayer which follows was given by a mother.

In Rebecca's home there were Mother, Daddy, an older sister Sue (who had had a toenail removed), a brother Alderson, and—best-loved of all—Grandmother.

One night Rebecca offered this prayer: "Bless Mother and Daddy, and bring Daddy safe home. Make Rebecca a good girl. Make Alderson a good boy. Put Sue a new toenail; and make Granny—no, leave Granny just like she is. She is all right."

Another incident which a mother confided brings a glow into our hearts:

It was Bobby's bedtime and he was very tired—so tired from a hard day's play that Mother let him skip the usual preparations for bed. She said, "We'll skip your bath, Bobby, and washing your teeth; you are so tired." Only the absolutely necessary things were done, and as she tucked the weary little boy under the cover and kissed him good-night, she said, "We'll have to skip prayers tonight, you are so tired," and then she turned out the light and left the room.

Hardly had she turned the knob of the door when a little voice called, "Mother, come back a minute."

As she stood again beside the bed, Bobby said, "I can't skip prayers tonight, Mother, 'cause He's gave me such a good day."

Incidents could be multiplied, if space permitted, to throw light on the big responsibility that belongs to parents and teachers—the responsibility of leading young children to commune with God.

Summary of Guiding Principles

It may not be necessary after our discussion to list the principles which should guide us in helping to develop the prayer life of children, but it may prove helpful to some of us to summarize what has been treated more or less in detail.

The following may suggest other principles which a church school teacher or parent may add:

1. Prayers worded for children should express their own experience.
2. In helping children to pray use very simple words.
3. Forms of prayer should be more beautifully expressed than if they were spontaneously expressed by the average child, and yet should be the child's own best thoughts.
4. Do not use the same form too often.
5. Help the children to understand that they may talk to God any time and anywhere.
6. Help the children to talk often to God in their own words.
7. Use the name "God" instead of "our Father" or "heavenly Father."

In the very discussion of the privilege and joy of leading children to commune with God, the responsibility causes a true teacher to bow in humble dependence and pray, "Lord, teach me how to teach these children to pray."

For Assignment and Discussion

1. Discuss "The Value and Danger of a Form Prayer."
2. Examine the two versions of the prayer below. Which do you prefer to use with little children? Why?

> "Now I lay me down to sleep,
> I pray Thee, Lord, my soul to keep;
> If I should die before I wake,
> I pray Thee, Lord, my soul to take."

> "Now I lay me down to sleep,
> I pray Thee, Lord, Thy child to keep;
> Thy love go with me all the night,
> And wake me with the morning light."

3. Check carefully your last Kindergarten session, or visit another church school Kindergarten, and note the opportunities which were used for worship. Were there any lost opportunities?

Helpful Books

Our Little Child Faces Life, Odell
Tell Me About Prayer, Jones
Teaching a Little Child to Pray, Milton
And When You Pray, McGavran
Guiding Children in Worship, Towner
Prayers for Little Children, Jones
My Bible Book, Janie Walker
My Prayer Book, Janie Walker

CHAPTER VIII

Listening to Stories

An Experience Which Aids the Religious Growth of Children

Listening to stories is one of the many activities which are used in the church school. There was a time when the story was felt to be "the lesson"; but now many activities are chosen to carry out the purpose of the session. At times there might be a session where no story was used because other experiences and activities could help to achieve the purpose better than a story could.

When to Tell Stories

A session with Kindergarten children should be informal and the story should be used when it fits naturally into the experience of the children. This may be the very first moment after the group has assembled, or perhaps at the end of the hour. Again it may be any time between.

Recall the experience of the children in "Picture Number One" in Chapter I. Note the place of the story in the experience. It was told at a time when the children seemed to be ready for it. It would have interested them, it is true, had it been told on their arrival, but the experience of trying to make a bird's nest would not have brought the desired results had it been preceded by the story. The children would not have had the experimental attitude that made them "try out" their ability to make a nest. Then, too, the feeling of awe and wonder which their experiment evoked made it easy for them to put themselves in Jimmy's place as he "had a look that eyes have when a person is thinking about God, and he said softly, 'Yes, it is wonderful!'"

One of the Bible stories which may be used with profit either as a preface to a discussion and dramatic play or as a climax to these activities is "A Room for a Friend."

After hearing the story the children may enjoy talking about and dramatizing "What I would do for a friend who comes to see me"; or, on the other hand, the story could be withheld until after the whole subject of friendly courtesy to guests has been discussed and dramatized, and then the group will enjoy hearing of the treatment which Elisha received from his friends. This particular type of story allows more freedom as to its place in the procedure than some others.

Whatever the story, the teacher should plan how it fits in with the other activities and be ready to use it when it will be most effective.

Selecting the Story

A story to be used with Kindergarten children should be suited to the age and understanding of four- and five-year-olds. It should be short. Usually it should not require more than five minutes for the telling, although there are exceptions to this rule. It should be simple, without too many complicated details and without long descriptions. It should not contain symbolism or abstract thoughts, as such things are beyond the understanding of this age. It should have action, for these children are active themselves and are interested in hearing of other children and people who do things. Only a story which contributes to the thought and purpose of the session should be used.

Preparing the Story

Read the Story

After the story has been selected, it should be read through a couple of times for pure enjoyment. Unless the story is appreciated by the teller, it is hardly possible that it will be appreciated by the listeners.

Next the story should be read again to gain the necessary knowledge about the characters and sequence of events.

Analyze

After this the story should be analyzed. Each story is divided into four parts: (1) The beginning; (2) Events leading to the climax; (3) The climax; (4) The conclusion.

1. *The Beginning.*

Some prefer the word "beginning" to the word "introduction" for the reason that most people understand that the "beginning" is a part of the story, whereas there are those who interpret the word "introduction" to mean something that is said by the storyteller before beginning the story.

Many stories are spoiled by being prefaced by explanations which are not at all needed. They are inartistic, and often they disclose facts which, given prematurely, strip the story of the element of suspense which is essential to a good story. There are storytellers who have learned not to "tack a moral" to the end of the story who still have not learned not to tack a preface to the story, for which they vaguely excuse themselves under the name "approach" or "introduction" or some similar word.

The following are illustrations of "tacking on a preface"—a most undesirable practice:

"I am now going to tell you a story about a man who was not afraid of lions."

"Should you like to hear a story about a little girl who helped a man?"

"We are going to listen to a story about Jesus helping a sick man."

Please remember that all of these are "prefaces tacked on"; they are not "beginnings."

A "beginning" gives the setting of the story and, as a rule, introduces the hero or heroine. If the time element is essential and the place important, they are a part of this setting.

Sometimes a "beginning" is one sentence only. Sometimes a number of sentences are needed to help the listener or reader visualize the setting. But it should never be long, for young children are eager for something to happen. The sentences should be short, and the imagery very concrete. This "beginning" should be a word picture which young children can easily understand and one in which they are really interested. If a "beginning" is uninteresting it is hard to induce the children to listen to the rest of the story.

The following is an example of a good beginning:

"Billy and Bobby were sitting on a doorstep wishing wishes."

2. The Events Leading to the Climax.

The second part of a story is the series or succession of events leading to a climax or high point in the narrative. A careful study of good stories will show each event leading up to the next, with no superfluous or ambiguous words, no misunderstanding of the order in which the events happened —a word picture in which the actors are clearly seen by their acts, with enough descriptive words to vitalize the events so that the reader or listener may visualize as clearly as though he were an eyewitness.

It is helpful in studying a story to list the events in their proper order, as a large part of the preparation for storytelling is a visualization (not memorization) of events.

3. The Climax.

The events, in their order, should always lead step by step to one outstanding event or high point in the story. We call this point the "climax." The story writer should have this high point in mind before he writes the story. In other words, he must know where he is going before he takes the first step. A well-built story is a work of art in which the climax tops the carefully built structure.

It is equally important that the storyteller know the climax before beginning to master the story. Telling a story without knowing the climax is like telling a joke without knowing the point. In each case the result will be a failure. It is true that it is quite possible for the climax of the story to be different for different age-groups or different occasions. The climax depends on the purpose that the storyteller desires to accomplish.

4. The Conclusion.

A young man in a storytelling class told a Bible story to the group. With the exception of one serious mistake he told it well. When the time came for criticism, after many words of commendation by the class, one student asked the teacher, "Would you have said, 'This teaches,' and then stated what the story taught?"

The teacher said, "No. We call that 'tacking on a moral.' If the story really did teach what B—— said it did, there was no need to say so. If it did not teach what he said it did, no words of his could make it do so."

The criticism was kindly given, and was received in a sportsmanlike manner, but the young man remained for a few minutes of explanation.

"Of course I knew better than to tack a moral on to my story," he said; "we have been talking about it all week. But it was this way—I was up there before the class and I had to stop and I did not know how, so I just kept on."

One can sympathize with his predicament, for perhaps the most difficult part of a story to handle is the conclusion.

It sometimes happens, but rarely, that the climax is also a proper conclusion. When that is the case, of course it is quite evident that the thing to do is to stop immediately after the climax has been reached. However, this is not often the case. In most stories a few words need to be added to give the reader or listener a sense of satisfaction—to set the mind at rest.

While a good conclusion is not a "tacked-on moral," it may be a means of emphasizing naturally that which will help the story to achieve the purpose for which it was told. For example, in the story, "God's Care of the Baby Moses," we might conclude with, "And many, many times, I know, the mother remembered to say 'Thank You' to God for helping her to take care of her little baby."

Visualize

After the story has been thoroughly analyzed, the teller should then think it through carefully, visualizing each scene.

Visualization does not mean a conscious memorization of the events or descriptive details of a story. The best storytellers do not memorize their stories. They see the word pictures so clearly that all they have to do is to tell to another what they see, and thus the telling becomes a joy.

Poor visualization results in a slovenly type of storytelling. Unprepared storytellers present to their hearers word pictures which are mere skeletons. The true storyteller is an artist who fills in all the necessary details, and with a touch of color here and there leads her hearers to see living pictures. We have no right to call ourselves storytellers when we are not willing to spend the needed time in accurate visualization. There is no excuse for slovenly storytelling, for anyone can learn to put into words an event which he sees clearly, and anyone, by concentration, can learn to see clearly the characters and events in a simple, well-constructed story.

Practice

Last of all, the storyteller must practice telling the story. This may be done silently at first, but it should always be done out loud at least once, for this gives confidence and shows the weak points in preparation that need to be strengthened.

All this preparation takes time, but when we realize that through our stories children are going to paint their own portraits of Jesus, or outline their own patterns of living, we are encouraged to put all necessary time into the mastery of stories.

Telling the Story

After the story has been well selected and carefully prepared there are certain principles which, if followed, will help to make the story a success with young children.

1. See that the children have had some activity before the story.

If the children have just had a long period of conversation or listening, they certainly will not be ready to continue sitting quietly for the story. Standing to sing or taking part in some relaxation activity will prepare them for better listening.

2. Seat the listeners comfortably and carefully.

At best it is difficult to hold the attention of a four- or five-year-old child. If little legs are dangling from chairs that are too high, the physical discomfort is apt to affect the reception of the story. See that chairs of the proper height are used.

If the children are crowded so that one child must touch another, there is a chance for divided attention. Before you begin your story see that each child has space enough to stretch his muscles, if necessary.

If the children are seated so that the storyteller has to make a decided effort to look into the eyes of all the listeners, interest is sure to lag.

There is no one way of seating a Kindergarten group which is acknowledged to be the only right way. In fact, it is well to have no cut-and-dried method, but from time to time to vary the method. There are times when the children may be seated in a semicircle; there are times when they may be seated in their chairs, informally grouped together in a rather compact group; and many teachers feel the best times of all are the times when they are seated happily on a big rug in an informal group, not close enough together for Tom to feel the necessity of kicking Ralph, in the effort to stretch his muscles, but near enough to feel cosy.

3. Try to secure the co-operation of the children before beginning the story.

Generally, if the stories told in the past have been interesting, the children are more than ready to listen when a story is suggested. Also, in the majority of cases the previous activities have so prepared and interested the children that the storyteller does not even have to say she is going to tell a story. She quickly notes that each child is attentive and she begins, "Many, many years ago in a land far away."

Often a good storyteller may start, even if one or two children are not listening, and proceed, depending on the interest of the story itself to gain their attention. However, sometimes if the group is inattentive, it may be necessary to say, "When everybody is listening, I shall tell the story."

4. Make use of direct discourse, contrast, and repetition.
Very often an inattentive child will become attentive to a story if direct discourse is used. A story that is colorless may be made to live through a method of visualization which brings the characters into bold relief. In the story of "Building a Room for a Friend," a child will not be so interested to hear you say, "The kind woman asked her husband if he did not think it would be a good thing to build a room on top of the house for Elisha"; as in hearing, "The woman said to her husband, 'Let us build a little room on the top of the house for him.'"

There is, however, a possibility of using too much direct discourse, thus making your attempt a dialogue rather than a story. Study carefully for a happy balance.

Contrast is a powerful method of helping the listener to see word pictures. Note in the following story the contrast between the disciples who were too busy to be bothered and the Friend of little children who was never too busy for any human need.

Jesus Loving Little Children

One day the people were crowding around Jesus when He was telling stories and making sick people well.

Everybody wanted to be near Him. They liked to hear Him talk. They liked to look into His eyes and liked to see Him smile.

Some of the mothers had brought their little children with them.

One of these mothers thought to herself, "I wish my little child could stand very close to Jesus—so close that He could take her up in His arms."

Another mother wished the same for her little child, and another mother wished it for her child. And so by and by the mothers began to take their children through the crowd closer and closer and closer to Jesus.

The friends of Jesus, His disciples, who stood near Him, said, "Don't bother Jesus with the children. He is busy. Take the children away."

But Jesus did not like it when they said, "Take the children away." His kind eyes looked into the eyes of the mothers and soon He was holding the little children in His arms, as He said, "Let the children come to me."* He put His hands upon the head of each child and blessed him.

This was a happy day for the mothers, and oh, such a happy day for the children!

Repetition is especially valuable in stories for Kindergarten children. It ranks with direct discourse in its power to catch and hold the attention. A familiar sentence or phrase is like a well-known friend in the midst of new associations, and is grasped eagerly by the listener. Repetition is always useful, if not overdone, and is most useful when it serves to emphasize the purpose for which the story is told. Examine the following story and note the use that is made of this teaching asset.

LOVE ALL THE TIME

Jim had learned a new Bible verse at vacation church school—"A friend loves at all times." When Mother asked him about the school, he said the verse for her, "A friend loves at all times." Little brother Teddy had just learned to talk and he always tried to say everything Jim did, but he couldn't quite get the words right, so he said, "Love all-a time." Then he made up a little song and started singing it, "Love all-a time, Love all-a time." It didn't have much tune but he went right on singing it over and over. Jim laughed, "That's a funny song." Teddy laughed too and sang it again. Mother smiled and said, "It's a good song, Teddy. And, Jim, that's a good verse to remember when you play with your friends. No matter what happens, you must show your love for them."

That afternoon Susan, who lived next door, came over to play and brought her cousin, Harry, who had come to see her. They had a good time for a while, then Harry said to Jim, "Let's go play something by ourselves. We don't want to play with girls!" This made Susan start to cry, and Harry said, "See, she's just a cry-baby!"

Just then little brother Teddy came around the house singing his song, "Love all-a time—Love all-a time." That made Jim think of the

---
* Mark 10:14. (R.S.V.)

Bible verse, "A friend loves at all times." So he said, "I want Susan to play with us, too. Let's go play in the sand pile."

Later, after Harry had left, Susan brought her new tricycle over and she said, "You ride your old trike, Jim, and I'll ride my new one." That was all right for a while, but Jim wanted to try out the new one, too. He asked Susan for a turn several times, but she wouldn't let him have one, and finally he said, "All right, if you won't share, you can take your trike and go home!"

Now Teddy was pulling his wagon around the yard and Jim could hear him singing at the top of his voice, "Love all-a time— Love all-a time." Jim thought, "Oh, that verse again! I'm sure not loving her now, but she ought to share." He thought for a minute and then he said, "I didn't mean for you to go home, Susan. You stay and we'll play." They played for a while and then Susan said, "Jim, you can ride my trike if you want to."

After supper that evening Daddy whispered to Jim, "Mother is so tired tonight. Let's surprise her and show her how much we love her by washing the dishes for her." But Jim wanted to see a certain television show and he said, "Oh, no, Daddy. Then I couldn't see my TV show." But just then he heard Teddy singing, "Love all-a time— Love all-a time." And right away he said, "All right, Daddy, I guess I can show Mother I love her all the time, too."

That night when Jim went to bed, he was singing softly to himself Teddy's little song, and Mother said, "I'm glad Teddy has been singing that because it surely helped you to remember that 'A friend loves at all times.'" Jim said, "It sure did," and he went to sleep singing it to himself, "Love all-a time—Love all-a time."

(The words "love all-a time" should be chanted to the same simple tune each time they occur.)

5. *Watch the tones of your voice.*

A good voice is a most valuable asset to a teacher, and should be cultivated as a part of her general preparation for teaching.

It will be difficult for any storyteller to improve her voice tones if she only gives thought to the voice while she is telling the story. Then, too, if undue thought is given at this time, there is likely to be an artificiality in the result.

A voice that is too loud is very unpleasant, and a story-teller who uses such a voice will not be able to convey different shades of meaning through contrasts in tone. These shades of meaning through voice tones should be spontaneous and natural—unstudied. There is nothing more objectionable than studied modulations which give the impression of a dramatic reading.

There is one exception to this rule of holding to natural voice tones. It is in the case of mimicking the sounds made by birds and animals. It really requires more practice than one would think to execute successfully the "meow" of the cat, the "bow-wow" of the dog, or the "ker-chunk" of a frog. The practice, however, is well worth while. Little children are very much more interested in Maud Lindsay's story, "Out of the Nest," when you say, "Brother bird listened and heard something down by the edge of the pond that went 'ker-chunk,'" instead of, "Brother bird listened and heard a frog croaking down by the edge of the pond."

Perhaps the storyteller will be discouraged at first by the flat sound that may result from her first attempt to make "ker-chunk" sound like a frog. Imagination and practice will produce a frog that at least is satisfying to this age-group.

The need for mimicry is not constant, but the tones of a natural, pleasing voice which can be distinctly heard are necessary for the enjoyment of a story by young children.

6. Use only natural gestures.

Gestures are a part of the person using them and should be perfectly natural and unstudied. Unnatural gestures, planned beforehand, will result in an artificial, wooden performance.

It is quite possible for a storyteller to use too many gestures, even though they are spontaneous. This indicates that too many gestures are in evidence in all her association with people; and the need for correction is a more general need than in its application to storytelling. She should endeavor in her everyday conversation to check, somewhat, her tendency to gesticulate, and her storytelling will profit by the general improvement.

7. Do not hurry your story.

It is hard to explain why a story suffers when the narrator does not feel that she has adequate time at her disposal—even though she omits no event—but it does. There is a hurried, breathless feeling that causes one to blur the word pictures, or to crowd the events one on the other in such a way that each does not stand out clearly. This does not mean that the story should drag. There is nothing more fatal to the success of a Kindergarten story than a slow, painful, dragging, uncertain style. Such a slow, painful style is not to be confused with a style that conveys the impression of ample time for the word pictures to be seen clearly—time enough even for a pause when necessary—an unhurried style which keeps the action moving swiftly and steadily.

8. *Do not say, "I forgot."*

When a mistake has been made do not say, "I forgot," but, if possible, cover up your mistake. There are times when the information you forgot to give is absolutely essential to the story and needs to be given, though delayed. Do so, but do not say, "I forgot." Sometimes the mistake can be covered so skillfully that the listener is not conscious of the former omission, but even if this is not the case, the statement, "I forgot," does not help.

9. *As a rule, do not ask questions.*

In most cases the storyteller should not ask questions during the telling of the story. Many a story has been spoiled by well-meant, supposedly harmless questions, the answers to which started a new train of thought in the minds of the listeners.

"What do you think?" is apt to bring irrelevant and undesirable answers.

There are occasional chances to emphasize a truth by the use of a question to which the answer must be "Yes." There is also a wise use of the question to which "No" will undoubtedly be the answer. This use of the question should be rare and always carefully considered beforehand. It is not possible in many stories to make this wise use of the question; therefore, the safest rule is to avoid asking questions in telling a story.

10. Learn to classify interruptions.

There are certain interruptions which should be ignored and certain others which, if correctly handled, may prove real contributions.

"I have some new shoes," in the midst of the story of "Jesus and the Children," should be ignored with a sympathetic smile, whereas, "I wish I had been there," may be recognized and accepted as a contribution. It takes quick thinking and good judgment to classify interruptions, but success is sometimes the result of quick thinking.

11. Forget yourself.

This is one of the most important rules for good storytelling. If the hearer sees you instead of the word picture you are attempting to portray, your story will be a failure, but if you lose yourself in what you are picturing, your story will be a vital factor in the lives of your hearers—a living pattern for right attitudes and conduct.

These storytelling "rules" or "principles" need not discourage amateurs. They sound more formidable than they really are. There are people who never read or heard a storytelling rule who tell stories well because they unconsciously obey the rules. There are many others, however, who only need a few suggestions to help them overcome mistakes of which they have not been conscious. If a story is a good story, it is worthy of our best efforts. No effort of ours should be too great if thereby children are guided into Christian conduct through the power of the story.

For Assignment and Discussion

1. What is the difference between visualization and memorization of a story?
2. Prepare a story suitable for use with four- and five-year-old children. Tell it to a group of children. Report as follows:
   What story did you tell? Why?
   How was the group seated?
   Did you have attention throughout?

How long did it take to tell the story?
What interruptions did you have?
What was the response of the children?
Did the story meet a real need of the children who heard it?

Helpful Books

The Storyteller in Religious Education, Brown
Education in the Kindergarten, Chapter XII, Foster and Headley, second edition.
Living in the Kindergarten, Chapter XV, Wills and Stegeman
Here and Now Story Book (Introduction), Mitchell

CHAPTER IX

Using Music

An Experience Which Aids the Religious Growth of Children

Just as music occupies a large part in the Christian worship of adults, so it holds an important place in the worship and lives of young children.

Selecting Songs

Songs are more widely used with the Kindergarten group than other forms of music, and certain principles should be remembered as guides in the selection of songs for these children.

1. The words of the song should be good.

The words of a song should be examined even before the music is tested, because no matter how good the music may be, cheap, jingly, trashy words should never be chosen.

The decision on whether or not the poetry is good will, of course, depend largely upon the taste of the person selecting the song. Good taste can best be cultivated by constantly living with the good.

Occasionally we find a song so simple that a four-year-old can sing it, and at the same time so great that it may be sung by a gray-haired man. This is perhaps rare, but such a song, I think, is the first stanza of Dr. Henry van Dyke's "Morning and Evening."

> "Every morning seems to say,
> 'There's something happy on the way
> And God sends love to you.' "[1]

Mrs. C. F. Alexander has given to many of us a sense of

---

[1] Used by permission Charles Scribner's Sons.

real satisfaction in her words (slightly adapted for young children):

> "All things bright and beautiful,
> All things large and small,
> All things wise and wonderful,
> Our God has planned them all!"

2. The words and ideas should be within the range of a child's experience.

Kindergarten children think in the concrete rather than the abstract, so the words of their songs must be about things they can see and hear and touch and know, instead of abstract things.

As stated before, children of this age do not understand the use of symbols. One young boy was lustily singing, "Brighten the corner where you are." When asked, "What does that mean?" he answered, "I don't know." When urged to think a bit, he finally said, "Well, I guess it is somebody talking to the sun." This shows he was giving the words a literal rather than symbolic meaning. The words of all songs should be examined carefully to be sure they will be understood by the children.

3. Words should have religious value and give correct ideas.

The songs that are used in the church school should have religious value and teach Christian principles. They should give a conception of God based on what we know of Christ.

4. The song should not be too long.

Usually the song should not be much longer than four lines, as it is hard for children of this age to concentrate on one song for any length of time. Each stanza should be short enough for them to make their own. In the case of a song of several stanzas it is often wise to use only one, which fills a present need, and add another later, as it may be needed.

5. The music should be good.

Children are beginning to form taste in music as in other things. Thus a teacher who helps to create a love for the best in music is making a real contribution to their development; and, what is more important, is providing a proper medium through which they may express their love for God and their thanks for His gifts. The best available music should be used for children's worship.

6. The music should interpret and enrich the words.

Bright, happy music should be sung to bright, happy words; and thoughtful music to thoughtful words. That is, the music should be suitable and harmonize with the spirit of the poem.

As an illustration, in the song, "The Children's Friend," the composer, Helen Howarth Lemmel, has caught the spirit of Miss Moore's lovely poem and given to us a most appropriate setting for the words, which tell one of the best-loved Bible stories. (See page 130.)

A Child's "Thank You"

Anonymous

ELDA FLETT BAKER

Joyously

Thank you for the world so sweet, Thank you for the food we eat,

rit.

Thank you for the birds that sing, Thank you, God, for ev - 'ry - thing.

The spirit of "Thank You" has been caught by the composer as she puts into melody "A Child's 'Thank You.'" The high note which voices the word "Thank" each time holds a world of joyousness. The repetition of the same tone each time serves to emphasize the thought that should be emphasized. There is a beautiful reverence conveyed in "Thank You, God, for everything."

7. *The harmony must be simple.*

Composers of music for four- and five-year-old children often make the mistake of clouding the melody of a song so that the children are confused and do not catch it readily. The songs are spoiled for children by the heavy style in which they are harmonized. They have an adult rather than a childlike quality. In the best songs for young children the melody stands out clearly, and the harmony, while good, is subordinated.

8. *The music must be within the range of a Kindergarten child's voice.*

This range is usually within the staff from first-line *e* to fourth-space *e*. This means that songs with many low notes or very high notes should not be used.

9. *The music should not be difficult.*

Perhaps, after all that has been said of simplicity of words and thought, it is not necessary to add this caution as to simplicity of music, but experience has shown that many of the songs that are taught to Kindergarten children should be classed as Primary songs, partly because of the difficulty of the music.

10. *The songs chosen should be suited to the thought of the session and should help to fulfill the purpose of that session.*

For instance, a nature song would not be used if the session was about the baby Jesus, neither would the song, "Jesus, Our Friend," be introduced if the lesson was about the boy Samuel.

If the purpose of the day is to help the children think of their families and what they can do for these families, songs such as "We Thank Thee for Our Happy Homes"[2] or

---

[2] From *When the Little Child Wants to Sing,* published by the Westminster Press.

"Prayer Hymn" which begins "Thank you, dear God, for our homes"[3] would be suitable to help carry out this purpose. However, one such as "When to Church I Go"[4] would not fulfill the purpose.

In the short time which we spend with our children in the church school let us choose songs that will be meaningful in their religious development. Let us choose songs that will be full of meaning as the children pause to sing them in their play, songs that will have real significance as they kneel to pray.

The Teacher's Collection of Songs

No one published songbook can possibly meet all the needs of a group of children, so the teacher should carefully compile a classified and indexed loose-leaf book which contains songs culled from books and other teaching literature. Such a book is very valuable, but more valuable still is the collection of songs stored in the leader's memory—songs that have become so much a part of her that, on a moment's notice, she can reach into her memory storehouse without waiting for the help of a pianist and bring out the song that exactly fits into the experience of the children.

Do not feel when you have collected songs designed to meet all the needs of children to which songs can minister that it is necessary for you to teach all of them during the two years which a child usually spends in a Kindergarten. Indeed, a small number of well-chosen songs mean more to the children than exposure to more than they can assimilate or make their own. Your complete loose-leaf book may be considered a valuable store of materials on which you can draw in time of need.

The songs selected from week to week should be chosen with your teaching purpose in mind. The lesson writer of

---

[3] From *When the Little Child Wants to Sing*, published by the Westminster Press (first line slightly adapted).
[4] From *Worship and Conduct Songs*.

your denominational lesson course always selects songs which she thinks should meet the needs and interests of most groups, but she does not mean to limit your choice to her choice. You will, as a rule, teach with more effectiveness a song of your own choice than one which someone else has chosen for you. It must be remembered, also, that no two groups of children respond in the same way. A response from a child may demand a song which the lesson writer could not foresee. As you choose your songs, keep in mind the rules given for the selection of songs, and remember they should help to fulfill the purpose of the session.

Using Songs

A thoughtful Kindergarten teacher was asked, "How do you teach songs to your children?" She replied, "I do not teach songs. I *use* them."

Of course she knows that using a song is teaching it, but her very phraseology makes us think. It makes a teacher know that she should not drill a song—that while repetition is needed before the children can make it their own, the repetition should be so motivated that the children will never feel the mechanics of learning.

There are several principles that may guide us in the use of songs.

1. Use the song to meet a real need of the children.

If this principle is kept in mind it will follow that no teacher will choose a song just "because it is pretty" or "because I like it" or even "because it is good." It will be chosen because she feels that by using that particular song she will be helping to enrich the experience of the children.

Children are sometimes afraid of the dark. They need to have pleasant associations with the nighttime developed or discovered. There are times when a song may help to do this. It will have its largest place of usefulness in the home, preferably at nighttime. Perhaps its next best place will be part of an imaginary experience at the church school. The children will have talked about the nighttime. Perhaps they will have looked at pictures like "Twinkle, Twinkle, Little Star" or "Moonbeams" or a picture of a child asleep. While their thoughts are pleasantly associated with the nighttime, the leader, without further introduction, will sing to them:

THE LITTLE NEW BIRDS ARE ASLEEP

The little new birds are asleep in the nest,
For their mother has cuddled them under her breast;
The night stars they twinkle and blink in the sky,
And the night wind is singing a lullaby—
Oo-oo-oo, lullaby.[5]

Over and over in the church school the children need to be guided to want to share with others. The following songs are useful to help meet this need. They may be sung by the teacher as she moves among the children during the playtime as well as during units on "Playing Together" or "Friends."

SHARING

Why not share a picture book?
Why not share a toy?
The thing you share with others
Is the thing that you enjoy.[6]

HAPPY PLAY

My friends and I have so much fun,
We share our toys with everyone.
We take our turns and laugh and play,
And have a happy, happy day.[7]

FRIENDS

Friends! Friends! Friends!
I have some friends I love!
I share my games and share my toys
With all my friends, both girls and boys.
Friends! Friends! Friends!
I have some friends I love! [8]

[5] From *Worship and Conduct Songs*, Shields.
[6] From *When the Little Child Wants to Sing.*
[7] From *Child Guidance*, January 1951.
[8] From *Worship and Conduct Songs.*

2. Build up a setting for a song, or, better still, use a natural setting that lends itself to the use of a song.

A group of Kindergarten children had been out in the churchyard searching for beautiful things God had made. They came in, ready to make an enthusiastic report. As, one at a time, they brought forward their discoveries, it seemed appropriate to introduce "The Wonder Song."

It is true the children had never heard it before, but the situation was so ripe for it that it simply sang itself. It was really another way of talking to each child to sing:

> "O, who can make a flower,
>   I'm sure I can't, can you?
> O, who can make a flower?
>   No one but God, 'tis true." [9]

Of course each discovery called for a slightly different wording. "Seed-pod," "red leaf," and "acorn" were substituted for the word "flower." By the time the song had been used conversationally with each child, the group had almost learned to sing it.

In informal teaching it is often difficult to say whether a situation is "built up" or "used." In the illustration just cited, doubtless it was "built up," because even before the teacher sent the children into the churchyard on their journey of discovery she anticipated to a certain extent the possible results and made the connection in her mind between the enterprise and the song which so aptly fitted into it.

There are, however, many times when a chance remark on the part of a child makes it possible to use a song at a time when it has not been planned. Such an opportunity came when David discovered a new picture and announced his discovery. It was a picture of some people standing in church singing. "I see we have a new picture," was his comment.

"What is the picture?" asked the teacher.

"It is people singing," was David's answer.

---

[9] From *Songs for the Pre-School Age,* Shumate. Published by S. S. Board of the Southern Baptist Convention. Used by permission.

"What do you think they are singing?"

" 'Praise Him,' " was the quick response of the children.

"I believe they are," said the teacher. "Perhaps we should like to sing it, too." And they did.[10]

3. Use each stanza of the song as a whole—never line by line.

Perhaps few of us are guilty of breaking up a song into lines, but there are still some teachers who have not learned to give to the children a whole word picture at one time. Such teachers would not cut Bouguereau's "Adoration of the Shepherds" into four sections, showing one at a time to the children, but they make the mistake of cutting up a song which tells the same story.

Baby Jesus

E. McE. S.
Gently

Melody by ELIZABETH McF. SHIELDS
Harmonized by HARRY S. MASON

1. On a bed of sweet, new hay. In a sta - ble far a - way Lit - tle Ba - by Je - sus lay fast a - sleep.
2. And His moth - er al - ways near, Cud - dled up the Ba - by dear, Lit - tle Ba - by Je - sus lay fast a - sleep.

Words used by permission Presbyterian Board of Christian Education
Music copyrighted, 1929, by Elizabeth McE. Shields

---

[10] It so happened that even though the teacher had not planned to use the picture at the time of its discovery, it fitted in quite well with the conversation then in progress, else her response might have been different.

They line out in singing:

> "On a bed of sweet, new hay"

and have the children sing it after them, followed by the next line:

> "In a stable far away."

And so the leader continues, little dreaming that she is destroying a beautiful word picture. Such procedure breaks all accepted laws of memorization as well as the laws of beauty.

4. Repetition should be rightly motivated—never drill. We have implied this principle, but it needs emphasis. Many times we are so concerned that the children shall be able to repeat all the words and sing the melody of a song that we have them sing over and over, forgetting that much more than rote repetition is involved in making a song one's own. It is better to take longer to teach it than to be satisfied with rote use of the words and music.

For example, we should seize suitable opportunities for singing prayer-sentences many times as prayers. The children will soon know the words, although they are never drilled. In this connection we should say that no prayer form, even in song, should be used too often.

Sometimes one song only may be used throughout an hour's session with the children—used many, many times with meaning.

Some children in a Kindergarten had been talking about their mothers and what they could do to help them. The teacher had sung:

> "When my father goes away,
> He says, 'Little brother,
> You must take my place today,
> Take good care of mother.'" [11]

Each child was allowed to sing the song with the leader. The children did not sense the fact that this repetition, which

---

[11] *Song and Play for Children*, Danielson and Conant, and *Songs for the Little Child*, Baker and Kohlsaat.

was perfectly natural to them, was helping them to learn the song. They were singing because it gave them joy.

It is interesting, however, to note that one little boy was able to sing the song perfectly at home in its proper setting,[12] even though his aunt who had visited his department during his learning experience could not remember it.

One opportunity for using the songs again and again so that they may become familiar and be made the children's own is an informal "sing" when the children may gather about the piano and choose favorites. This is often a happy activity of the children who arrive early.

There are many ways of using songs without drilling them. The wise teacher will recognize the value of repetition, but will motivate it.

5. Vary the ways of using songs.

While children love the familiar and it is well frequently to do what has been done before, it is not wise to become monotonous in our teaching. If pictures have been used a great many times to introduce songs, it will be well to vary the procedure and build up an appreciation through conversation or through creative work, if the song lends itself to one of these methods. A resourceful teacher will not allow her method to become monotonous. Neither will she move restlessly from one method to another so frequently that there is no feeling of stability.

6. Encourage the children to sing in their natural voices— not in loud tones.

Many little children have strained their voices by singing in loud tones. They can be led to sing sweetly and naturally if the leader sings naturally and softly. We should remember that young children have soft voices—that the singing of four- and five-year-old children, technically speaking, is not calculated to impress the listener as a wonderful vocal achievement. But the children can be led to express themselves in a few songs that will be pleasing to themselves and

---

[12] His Daddy left town for a few days.

to God, and that will be appreciated by those who understand this avenue of expression.

7. *As a rule, introduce words and music together.*

There is no iron-clad rule which makes it absolutely
wrong to separate words and music at times, but, as a rule,
they should not be separated. This does not mean that the
music to a song may not have previously been used as quiet
music.

For example, you may have decided to help to give the
children an appreciation of Jesus' love for children. You
plan to use the story "Jesus Blessing Little Children," and
Plockhorst's picture of the story. You search your songbook
and find the simple and beautiful song by Jessie Eleanor
Moore, which both pictures the event and portrays the love
of Jesus today for children. But—the song is new, the children have not heard it before.

Words and music will not really be separated if the music,
with no particular comment, is played as quiet music by the
pianist. Perhaps she will play the music a second time so

The Children's Friend

JESSIE ELEANOR MOORE   HELEN HOWARTH LEMMEL

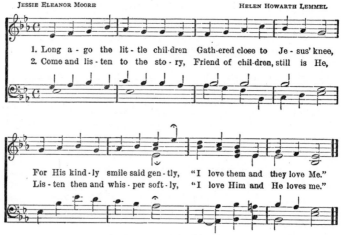

1. Long a - go the lit - tle chil-dren Gath-ered close to Je - sus' knee,
2. Come and lis - ten to the sto - ry, Friend of chil-dren, still is He,

For His kind - ly smile said gen - tly, "I love them and they love Me."
Lis - ten then and whis - per soft - ly, "I love Him and He loves me."

Copyright, 1920, by Jessie Eleanor Moore

that the melody will be absorbed by the children unconsciously. Then, when it seems exactly suitable, after the story has been told and the picture used, you may say, "I feel like singing about the picture," and sing, without the piano, "The Children's Friend."

Then it will be quite natural after the words have been sung to the children to say, "Miss .... knows how to play on the piano the story I have been singing. Perhaps you would like to listen as she plays it for us."

Then you will sing it with her as she softly plays it again. You may invite the children to come up, a few at a time, and stand close to the picture while you sing the song for each group. Possibly you will not use the piano at all for a while, but in any case you will sing the words rather than say them, and you will encourage the children to join you as they wish.

8. Usually the first introduction of a song should be without an instrument.

In most cases the children should be introduced to the song by hearing it sung by the leader without an instrument. In this way they accept the fact that their teacher is "telling" them something even though her medium of expression is the singing voice, instead of the talking voice. The piano is apt to cloud the words and bring more formality into the introduction. Afterward the pianist may accompany the children in singing songs of a certain type. There are, however, many songs of a conversational type which should, in most cases, be sung without the piano. In fact, many children sing best without accompaniment.

9. Songs may be sung to the children for their enjoyment.

Because there is so little time in the church school session, Kindergarten children cannot learn to sing very many songs, yet often a teacher knows she can enrich their experience through a song which they can readily understand and appreciate, but which it will take too long to master. It can make its emotional appeal or give certain valuable information, even though she does not expect the children to be able to sing the words. "Sleeping and Waking Seeds" is such a song.

Creating or Adapting Songs

Many times a song does not exactly suit the experience through which the children are living, but slight changes or adaptations, or even an added stanza, will meet the situation. Until a teacher has made an effort at adaptation she may not realize her own ability and initiative.

A skillful teacher of Kindergarten children made a beautiful adaptation of the song, "A Child's 'Thank You.'" (See page 121.) She was building up an appreciation of the wonderful and beautiful things God has made. Her children, under two competent assistants and herself, had spent some time at three tables examining and talking about God's creations. One group was particularly interested in the scattering of the seeds by the wind. Another was looking at an acorn that had taken root, from which a tiny oak tree was beginning to grow. The third was examining birds' nests and talking about birds. The leader then called them together and welded their experiences and gave them a chance to thank God through the following adaptation of a prayer-song which included the three experiences:

"Thank You for the winds that blow,
Thank You for the trees that grow,
Thank You for the birds that sing,
Thank You, God, for everything."[13]

Adults do not do all the creative work in children's music. Occasionally Kindergarten children "make up" very simple words and melodies.

A Musical Instrument

Where it is possible, a piano should be in the Kindergarten room. But if a piano is too costly, an organ should not be

[13] Adapted from "A Child's 'Thank You.'"

used just because there is one handy. An organ clouds the melody, making it difficult for children to follow.

Teachers should realize that it is quite possible to use songs effectively with children without a piano. Indeed, there are many teachers who should use the piano much less than they do. Very often the informality of the song is spoiled by having to wait for the pianist, and sometimes the instrument seems to come between the simple, sympathetic song-story and the children.

Instrumental Music

Ordinarily, young children will not listen to instrumental music for any length of time, but they can be helped to listen, and gradually music will have meaning for them as a means of expressing joy, quiet reverence, and other emotions.

They need guidance in their listening. The question may be asked, "How does that music make you feel?" or "Let's see if Miss .... can make the piano sound like bells." Often listening to a soft lullaby will help a group to become quiet.

Instrumental music can also be used as rhythms to encourage the children in certain activities such as flying like birds, swaying like trees in the wind, or growing like flowers.

If the Kindergarten has access to a record player, records can be found which will be within the appreciation of the children and which will help to carry out the purpose of the session.

The Pianist

The pianist needs to be a good musician—one who understands children and children's music. She needs to remember that the pianist is as truly a teacher as the other assistants, and should be ready to fit into the experiences of the children. She may not always know just what song the leader will call for, since in the informal way of teaching even the leader herself does not always know when a song will be needed.

It is true, however, that on account of the informality in most cases it is perfectly in harmony with the procedure to say, "Miss ...., will you play the song about when Jesus was a baby boy, or "Miss ...., do you know a song about friends?" This takes any feeling of strain from her and makes for a sympathetic understanding between leader and pianist.

In order to do this effectively, it will be helpful if the pianist has a memory "storehouse" of the songs and instrumental music used frequently with the children, or at least knows where she can turn to the needed music on a moment's notice.

A good Kindergarten pianist is a rare treasure. It is to be hoped that more good musicians who love little children will use their talents to help these children to express themselves truly and beautifully in song.

For Assignment and Discussion

1. Is using a song teaching it? Prove your answer by one or more of the laws of learning found in Chapter II.

2. Examine your teaching literature and note the various methods employed in the use of songs.

3. If you observe or work with a group of children over a period of several weeks, keep a careful record of the number of times a given song was used before the children had made it their own.

Helpful Books

Music in the Religious Growth of Children, Shields
There's Music in Children, Sheehy
Living in the Kindergarten, Chapter XI, Wills and Stegeman
When the Little Child Wants to Sing, Laufer
Song and Play for Children, Danielson and Conant
A Little Book of Singing Graces, Brown
Music in Christian Education, Thomas

CHAPTER X

Other Experiences Which Aid the Religious Growth of Children

Play

Living for little children means playing. It has been said that a young child's day may be divided into two parts—routine, which takes in the necessary things such as eating, bathing, dressing, sleeping, etc., and play which takes in everything else.

Play is a child's natural way of learning. Through play he reproduces activities he has seen or heard about; he experiments with materials and equipment, gaining muscular control, courage, a sense of achievement; he is helped to gain emotional control and to meet new situations; he develops Christian skills, such as consideration for others, learning to share and take turns.

Because play is so important to children and because it is through this activity of play that they learn best, some of the most effective teaching in Kindergarten is done as the children are playing. The teacher can observe individual attitudes and interests; she can give religious guidance to the play by suggesting ways of sharing and activities of helping, relating it all to God and the familiar verses of the Bible. Thus the children learn to be friendly and helpful and to show love. These "learnings" become actual experiences in Christian living. They may "learn" the Bible verse, "Be kind to one another," so that they can say it perfectly, but until they have had a chance to practice ways of being kind over and over, they have not learned it well enough to live it.

Through play they will have also many happy associations with the church, which is one of the goals toward which we are striving in the religious education of our children.

Informal Play

This play, which means so much to the children, should be creative, and may be supervised, but not directed, by the teachers. The teachers may make suggestions to help the play to be more creative or to bring other children in; and they may supply extra materials which may be needed; but they should never "take over" the play, as this causes the children to lose interest.

Certain toys should be provided for this type of play. No mechanical toys have any place in Kindergarten—only those which can be used creatively by the children, such as large building blocks, farm animals, trucks, cars, dolls, doll beds, tea table, and dishes. See "Play Center Furnishings" in Chapter V. With such things the children dramatize everyday experiences and many new ones, learning co-operation and helpfulness as they do so.

Dramatic Play

Along with this informal play there is also dramatic play and the two are often interchangeable. At first, perhaps, a child is hauling blocks rather aimlessly in a truck to make some sort of a building; then suddenly in his imagination the truck becomes an ambulance—he has become an ambulance driver, the block building is a hospital; and soon several others are drawn into the dramatic play of hospital life.

A certain type of dramatic play is often suggested by the teacher if some new experience is being planned; and the children will "play" how they will present a gift or how they may show kindness to visitors.

Story Play

Children of this age do not often act out whole stories. But they do enjoy playing certain incidents of well-known stories. However, they usually leave the talking of the characters to the teacher.

Rhythmic Play

Most children enjoy rhythmic play. This can be accompanied by music or singing or just speaking, and it provides activity and change of position which young children need often. Such rhythms, when used, should fit the thought and purpose of the lesson if possible, but often the teacher needs something to use just for relaxation and stretching. The following are a few such plays which can be used. The actions should suit the words.

OPEN, SHUT (*using hands*)

Open, shut, open, shut
　And give a little clap.
Open, shut, open, shut
　And lay them in your lap.

TAP AND CLAP (*standing*)

Let your feet go tap, tap, tap;
Let your hands go clap, clap, clap;
Let your head nod to and fro;
Round and round and round we go. (*Turning around*)

SMALL AND TALL

Sometimes I'm very, very small; (*Stooping low*)
Sometimes I'm very, very tall; (*Stretching high*)
　Now I'm just right. (*Standing straight*)

Singing instructions such as "It's time to clean up now," to a tune like "Farmer in the Dell," or "It's time for everybody now to come to me," to simple tunes like "London Bridge" or "Mulberry Bush," encourages the children to obey and do things together.

A few suggestions for rhythms are given in Chapter IX, "Instrumental Music."

Using Visual Materials

Visual materials include many things, such as pictures, books, models, objects, filmstrips and slides.

Pictures

A Kindergarten teacher uses pictures more often than any other visual materials. Picture sets are included in the teaching materials of the various denominations and these of course may be used to achieve the purpose of the lessons.

The teacher should always be on the lookout for useful pictures from magazines and other sources. These should be simple and without too many details. They should portray action and be of interest to a child. They should be within the understanding of children and therefore should not be symbolic in any way.

All the pictures used in the Kindergarten are much more attractive if mounted on colored construction paper or lightweight cardboard so that they will stand handling. Some teachers keep a supply of cardboard frames of different colors into which can be slipped the large teaching pictures as they are needed. One caution—these frames should be plain colored cardboard, not all fancied up with designs or crepe paper, as this takes away from the picture itself. The mountings and frames should be of a color that will harmonize with the colors in the picture to be used.

The pictures should be filed in a manner which will keep them safe but easy to find, and they should be classified according to subjects so that they can be found immediately when needed. (See topic, "File for Mounted Pictures," in Chapter V.)

Smaller pictures will be needed often for use by the children in making posters or scrapbooks, and the wise teacher will constantly add to her classified collection all such pictures which she can find and which she thinks may be useful. Any old Sunday school materials should be kept and classified according to subjects, as these pictures will be in demand often in many activities.

Using Pictures

In order to stimulate the children's thinking and conversation, each Sunday pictures which relate to the thought of the session should be placed on the picture rail or tacked on the bulletin board. All the pictures, whether on rail or board, should be placed at the eye level of the children.

These pictures will probably be noticed by some of the boys and girls during the period of early activities, and a teacher should be near at hand to help these children to enjoy them. During the come-together time when the children are seated in a semicircle facing the teacher, she may refer to the pictures in various ways to bring them to the attention of the children.

The special large teaching picture for the day (from the denomination's materials) may either be prominently displayed on the beauty center table or be kept behind the table to be shown at the end of the story, if it pictures the story. Many teachers prefer this latter method of showing the picture after telling the story, since the children's attention is distracted from the story if the picture is shown during the telling. Of course there are exceptions to this rule; for instance, if a picture narrative is being told, parts of the picture will have to be pointed out in the telling; or if the picture shows objects with which the children are not familiar and the meaning of the story might be lost if they do not understand these objects. An illustration of this might be the story of Rebekah drawing water from the well for the camels of Abraham's servant. Here it might be necessary for the children to visualize the well and even perhaps the camels.

In many small church schools the large teaching pictures are not made available, but the same pictures in small size may be found in the children's materials. The teacher should cut these out and mount them on harmonizing colors of construction paper or cardboard so they may be used in the same way as the large pictures mentioned above.

Picture Books

Books for the children should be carefully chosen. The pictures should be simple and should appeal to the interest of a child as well as be within his ability to understand. Children enjoy books which are not too large. Those of a size of eight by eight inches or thereabouts seem to be easy for them to handle. The teachers' guides usually give suggestions about books suitable for use with each unit.

Objects

Many objects will be used to aid the teaching in the Kindergarten. Flowers, leaves, seed pods, old birds' nests, old wasp nests, cocoons, shells, fruit, vegetables, and other objects of nature can all be used to stimulate interest in God's out-of-doors. A model of an Oriental house made from a large box upon which a smaller box can be placed for an upper room helps the children visualize the living quarters of the people in Bible times. Objects from other countries which the children can understand will help develop a missionary spirit of friendliness.

Using the Bible

Every Kindergarten group should have a Bible and it should be used every Sunday by the teacher. In the lesson materials there are suggested verses to be used with the children, and these should be read from the Bible. The verses which it is hoped the children will learn should be used often during the sessions—not as drill, but in many different ways so the children will become familiar with them and so they may become a part of the children's living. Often the boys and girls will enjoy holding the Bible as they "read" the verse. The words of the Revised Standard Version can usually be better understood than those of the King James Version. Whenever a Bible story is told, the teacher should hold the Bible in her lap and make sure the children understand the source of the story.

If a Bible which has pictures in it is to be chosen for use in the Kindergarten, one should carefully check the pictures to see if they are suitable for these children to see.

Many teachers cut the picture from the pupil's material,

mount it on white paper just the size of the page of the Bible and place it in the Bible where the story for the day is found. This makes it quite interesting to the children.

The Offering and Other Gifts

Offering

Since youngsters four and five years old cannot be expected to hold on to their money for any length of time, a place should be provided where they may put it soon after they enter the room. Most teachers agree that this should not be at the door, since the children may get the feeling that they are paying to enter the room. The best place for the basket or container in which they may place their money seems to be on the table in front of where the whole group comes together. Some call this table a beauty center or a worship center. Here can be placed the Bible, the offering basket, and a vase of flowers. As each child comes in the door he is greeted and invited to this spot to place his money in the basket, then he goes to take off his wraps before looking around for some play or work activity.

When the whole group comes together this offering should be dedicated in some simple way. One child may be asked to stand by the teacher and hold the basket. (Incidentally, a careful list should be kept of the ones chosen so that everyone may have a turn. Even though there are only six or eight in a class and the teacher is sure she can remember who has done it, there is no use taking a chance of hurting someone's feelings, and writing it down assures fairness for all.) There should be a conversation about where the money will be used, stressing the fact that part is used to pay expenses in the church school—the lights, the church school papers, the services of the janitor; and some is used to help new Sunday schools, and send papers and pictures to boys and girls who do not know about Jesus. Then perhaps a simple offering song or a verse may be used and a prayer. Be sure all the words used in the song or verse or prayer are within the understanding of the children.

Friendly Gifts or Enterprises

Often the children are guided to desire to do something for others, such as bringing food at Thanksgiving and toys at Christmas for needy people; making scrapbooks for children in a hospital ward; mounting pictures of Jesus for use by missionaries. When these gifts are brought or completed they should be dedicated in a simple way through conversation and prayer.

Excursions or Trips

Many times the children are taken on short walks or trips when such excursions will further the purpose of the session. If they are thinking together about the church, a quiet walk through the church sanctuary will stimulate their interest and a short church service will help develop an attitude of reverence. If there is a nature unit, how could they better learn than by going out of doors to see and hear and touch and smell some of the things of beauty God has created? If they have made a gift for a shut-in who lives near the church, they might go to deliver the gift and sing a song or two. If they have been talking about community helpers, they might visit the firemen in a near-by station or a friendly policeman. Such trips or excursions promote real religious growth, as the children gain much more by doing and seeing for themselves than by sitting and talking about things.

Related Handwork Activities

There are many times when handwork will be used creatively. This will never be for mere busywork, but only when it will specially carry out the purpose of the session. It should not be used unless it is either an outgrowth of the experiences the children are having or will help to interpret the experiences they are ready to have, and unless it is within their ability and understanding.

If the children have been talking about God's beautiful springtime and they get down on the floor before a long piece of shelf paper to draw a mural of some of the beautiful things God has made, their thoughts are being focused on these things through their activity.

If the topic of the session is "Families" and the children are guided to draw pictures of their own homes before the come-together time, these same pictures may be used as a basis for stimulating conversation about their families.

Often posters can be made on which the children draw or paste pictures of certain subjects, such as: Ways our money gifts are used; Ways we grow; Friendly helpers; How we can be friendly (according to the topic for the day); and these posters may be used as bases for discussions or as summaries of conversations. This sort of creative drawing and postermaking aids the children in thinking constructively about things that help them grow religiously.

Making simple gifts for members of the family, friends, sick children in the hospital, children of other lands, or other groups in their own church, helps in the development of Christian traits in the Kindergarten boys and girls.

Certainly handwork should not be used every Sunday, because other activities are just as important or more so. But when it can help in the attainment of the purpose of the lesson in the thoughts and lives of the children better than some other of the activities; and when it can be used creatively—never just coloring within the outlines; and when the children can really understand it—what and why they are doing; then it should be used, and it will be of real value in the religious training of the children.

For Assignment and Discussion

1. Report an actual experience of co-operative dramatic play (not story play) among a group of children and note the following:

Was it teacher-inspired or child-inspired?
How many children were drawn into it?
What part did the teacher take?
Do you feel the children "learned" anything from it?
Have you any suggestions showing where the teacher might have helped in a better way?

2. Make a list of the subjects which might be used in the classification of a file for pictures for Kindergarten. For instance, for the Bible pictures work out several classifications under the general divisions of Stories of the Old Testament, Life of Jesus, Other New Testament Stories. Do the same for the pictures which do not pertain to the Bible.

Helpful Books and Pamphlets

PLAY:

Experiences in the Church School Kindergarten, Moore (In process of revision)

Education in the Kindergarten, second edition, Chapter XI, Foster and Headley

Living in the Kindergarten, Chapter XIII, Wills and Stegeman

Guiding the Young Child, Chapters V and VI, edited by Heffernan

PICTURES AND BOOKS:

Experiences in the Church School Kindergarten, Moore

Education in the Kindergarten, second edition, Chapter XII, Foster and Headley

OFFERINGS AND GIFTS:

Experiences in the Church School Kindergarten, Moore

MANY OTHER ACTIVITIES:

Teaching Kindergarten Children, Chapters V and VI, Gardner

Teaching Four and Five Year Olds, Chapter VII, Bickel

Portfolio for Kindergarten Teachers, Association for Childhood Education, Washington, D. C.

CHAPTER XI

Planning and Carrying Out Informal Procedure

Elements of a Program

In every Sunday session we hope we may guide the children to worship, to have fellowship together, to acquire knowledge, and to form a desire to live a little better life because of this time spent in the church school. All these elements are so interwoven that they cannot be separated from one another. Worship may result from friendliness and from the acquiring of knowledge, or it may be a part of both of these elements. Friendliness may result from worship and from the acquiring of knowledge. Knowledge may be gained through worship and through a friendly sharing. And so all are interrelated.

Worship

As we plan our procedure we know that the element of worship should have a very important place. So many things make or mar the atmosphere that should be conducive to worship. The appearance of the room, the attitude of the leader and helpers, the manner of introducing the songs, stories, play, and pictures, and the very tones of voice in voicing prayers, all make an impression on a child, making it either natural or difficult for him to worship.

A formal set service is not conducive to worship. It must be remembered that a child cannot be forced to worship. Often a head bowed and pious words repeated do not mean communion with God at all. Rather, opportunities must be seized when the responses of the children show they are ready for worship.

We must plan for moments of worship in every session and, in the planning, try to imagine where the appropriate time will come. For instance, if an active game were to be used as a relaxation activity, one would not try to place a prayer after it. On the other hand, if the whole session had been about playing together in a Christian way, and if after a story and discussion the children had experienced a time of playing in such a manner, they could be led to think about thanking God for such a happy time and for helping them to remember how to play as He wants them to do.

Very carefully we should plan what method we will use to try to guide the children to a feeling of worship—whether this time would come best after a story or a conversation or the showing of a picture, or perhaps after using a Bible verse. We should think of just how we will suggest it, of what responses the children might make, of how we could use those responses to bring them closer to God. Then during the actual session it may be that the children will be ready for worship just when we have planned it; but if they are not ready, we must go on with the session, watching carefully for an opportunity when it will mean something to the children.

The following is an illustration of how a time of planned worship was discarded for spontaneous worship which meant more to the children.

A group of teachers were planning a session about "God's Gifts in Spring," with the purpose of helping the children to see evidences of God's love and care in the springtime world and of guiding them to feel and express their gratitude to Him for His springtime gifts. The teachers were following the plans suggested in the leader's guide. They arranged to bring many spring flowers which the children might place in vases when they first arrived. Since a new song, "All Things Bright and Beautiful," was to be introduced, they decided to let the children make a picture poster about it. They collected suitable pictures to illustrate the phrases of the song. They worked out a session procedure in outline form, as follows:

Arranging flowers by some children.

Making of the song poster by some of the children; the teacher talking with them about the song and helping to choose the right pictures to paste on the poster.

All children gather together.

Song—"All Things Bright and Beautiful"—to be introduced by using the poster.

Conversation about things mentioned in song, the children naming many different things—using song often during conversation.

Using Bible verses:

"The flowers appear on the earth." (Song of Solomon 2:12a.)

"The time of the singing of birds is come." (Song of Solomon 2:12b.)

"We give thanks to thee, O God." (Psalm 75:1a, R.S.V.)

Prayer—let children help make a litany, using the verse of thanks, "We give thanks to thee, O God," as they name beautiful springtime things.

Song—"All Things Bright and Beautiful."

Dramatizing flowers growing—children crouching down like seeds in ground, growing, slowly rising and finally spreading out arms.

Story—"Sunshine and Rain"—a modern child-life story of a growing garden which needed sun and rain, ending with the thought of the children's joy because God had planned for sunshine and rain to help their gardens grow.

Prayer—thanks to God for sunshine and rain.

Drawing things to be seen in the springtime.

Conversation about drawings.

Song—"All Things Bright and Beautiful."

Dismissal.

As the teachers planned for the first prayer in the session, they hoped to lead the children to a feeling of joy and praise to God for beautiful things while using the Bible verse as a refrain in the litany prayer. They felt that at the end of the story perhaps their children could join with the story children in a feeling of gratitude for God's plan for sun and rain.

During the actual session on Sunday, things proceeded very much as planned. They were conversing about the things mentioned in the song, and when the song poster was shown there was a picture of butterflies illustrating small things. As this picture was pointed out, one child jumped up to tell how he had seen a butterfly come out of a cocoon. All the children were interested and when he had finished, the leading teacher supplied more information and showed a picture of a cocoon and a butterfly, which she had asked one of the helpers to find in the picture file. The children were thrilled, and one boy said softly, "You mean butterflies come out of things like that?" And the teacher said, "Yes, isn't it wonderful that God has planned for caterpillars to make cocoons, go to sleep inside them, and then wake up butterflies? I would like to tell Him how glad I am." She bowed her head to voice a simple prayer and every child there seemed to experience a feeling of wonder and worship.

That special moment had not been planned ahead of time, but the teacher was wise enough to grasp it when it was presented. And there certainly was more of a feeling of worship than might have been possible with the litany as first planned. The litany was omitted after the Bible verses, but the prayer at the end of the story was well placed, for, just as the story was finished, one girl said, "Let's thank God for the sunshine and rain like Mary and Bobby did." And before the teacher could say a word, most of the children bowed their heads and several said, "Thank you, God, for the sunshine and rain," and one said, "I'll be glad for the rain when it rains next time, God."

Always we should be on the lookout for times when we can help the children to feel their nearness to God. Several more illustrations of such times are given in Chapter VII where spontaneous prayers are discussed.

Fellowship or Friendliness

The element of friendliness or sharing should have a large place in our plans. It should be evidenced by a courteous welcome to new pupils and absentees, by a friendly sharing of experiences in happy talk, by sympathetic thought for members of the group or church friends who are sick or in trouble, by thoughtful recognition of happy events in the lives of these same friends, and by sharing work and play materials.

The expressions of friendliness may be and should be in most cases incidental. In the case of a new pupil, much will depend upon the pupil. If he is timid, he will not want to be singled out for too much special attention. Sometimes a courteous recognition from the teacher is all that is needed.

A word of welcome to the returned absentee is sufficient. The children may be led to show special consideration for such a one, as well as the new pupil, by waiting turns and by foregoing special privileges in his favor.

Birthdays of the children are among the very happiest events which furnish an opportunity for developing the friendliness of the group. The celebration of a birthday is a part of the procedure which may be planned in advance, as the teacher, of course, has a record of all the birthdays in her group. Children dearly love to have the postman bring letters to them. For this reason the birthday card may be mailed.

The celebration in the church school should be simple. Sometimes a birthday song is sung and always a birthday prayer is appropriate. An informal prayer like the following may be voiced by the teacher: "Dear God, we thank You for Betsy. We are happy with her on her birthday. Amen."

The arrival of a new baby in one of the church homes is an event which only needs to be announced to cause a spirit of friendliness to radiate toward "Mary who has a new baby brother."

In addition to the many everyday opportunities for friendliness, there are special days such as Christmas, Thanksgiving, and Easter when the children may engage in some enterprises that may bring much happiness to them and to the recipients. Sometimes a contact may be made with "faraway" friends with picture cards and messages.

Many teachers who recognize the value of cultivating a spirit of friendliness have failed to make use of the most natural means at hand of helping to develop this spirit—that is, the sharing of work and play materials. It is well to remember that one of the most important reasons for including these materials in our curriculum is that through their use a spirit of Christian friendliness may be fostered.

Acquiring Knowledge

There must be in our plans a provision for helping our children to acquire the right kind of knowledge. As we have said, this knowledge will best come as a part of all the activities of the hour, but there must be a conscious effort on the part of the leader to help the children to "know." They must know the nature of God before they will desire to worship Him. They must know what Christian friendliness is before they can practice it. And so the child comes to know or get a pattern of Christian living through the use which he makes of stories, poems, verses, pictures, certain types of songs, dramatization and other creative work, and enterprises of various kinds.

Desire for Better Living

Throughout the participation in these other elements of the program and as a result of them, we hope there will be a desire within each child to make a change in his way of acting. To accomplish this, we plan, where possible, actual opportunities which will give him experiences of acting in this changed way. If this is impossible, the next best plan is for him to dramatize or pantomime such experiences. For we must remember it is only as he has a chance to try out these things many times that they will become a part of his living.

Steps in Planning Procedure

Throughout this book informal methods of procedure have been stressed. This does not mean that the teacher will not have made plans for the session. But it does mean that the plans she has made should be elastic, to be modified by the responses of the children.

In the teaching materials furnished by the denominations the lesson writer usually has planned a well-balanced procedure to meet the needs of the average group. These plans will often need to be adapted, but they should be studied carefully and followed by teachers who have not had much experience in informal teaching.

The following steps in program planning may serve to show how to work out an informal procedure ahead of time.

1. Consider carefully the purpose for the day.

The purpose is most important because all the activities to be chosen will be measured by their value in fulfilling the purpose. This purpose is based upon the specific needs of children and consists of what we hope will take place in each child's thinking and feeling and acting during and after the session. This purpose, of course, must be formulated in the light of the goals for the Christian education of children as discussed in Chapter I.

The purpose is always stated at the beginning of every lesson in the denominational teacher's materials. If you are not following a teacher's guide, but are working out your own procedure plans, remember that the purpose for the lesson must not grow out of your desire to tell a certain story to the children, but must grow out of a real need of the children.

As you start planning, jot down the purpose, perhaps in outline form, so that you can see it clearly in all its parts.

As an illustration, let us suggest for a session's purpose: To help the children grow in their understanding of how to be friendly and in their desire to be friendly; and to provide opportunities for them to show love and consideration for others as God wants them to do. In this session we want the children to make a change in their way of thinking (we want them to think and to know how to be friendly and that God wants them to do this); in their way of feeling (we want them to desire to be friendly to others); and in their way of acting (we want to give them opportunities where they can actually show friendliness to others).

2. With the purpose in mind, list all of the various activities which could help to accomplish this purpose.

Of course you will not expect to use all the materials and

activities listed. The list is to enable you to choose the best available activities which will help to accomplish your purpose.

Continuing with the illustration of an informal procedure which was started above, let us list all the activities and materials we might use in developing a session with the suggested purpose.

Songs—any which bring out the idea of friendliness, such as, "Friends" or "Happy Play" or "A Happy Day."

Bible verses:

"Forget not to show love." (Hebrews 13:2a, a.s.v.)

"Love one another." (John 13:34b.)

"A friend loves at all times." (Proverbs 17:17a, r.s.v.)

Story—Jonathan and David from Bible, or some modern child-life story based on the Bible verse, Hebrews 13:2a.

Pictures—David and Jonathan if that story is used; pictures of children playing together, illustrating different ways of playing happily.

Worship—thanking God for play experiences; asking for help to remember to be friendly.

Other activities—conversation about being friendly; pantomiming play experiences; dramatizing situations when children come to play; actual play experiences.

3. Consider the time at your disposal, the necessity for frequent change of activity, the inability of young children to master too much new material, and then select only those activities which in your judgment will best accomplish your purpose.

While Sunday, weekday, and vacation school programs may avail themselves of the same type of activities, using practically the same materials, a choice of activities must be made largely on a time basis. For example, the session of a vacation school is, as a rule, longer than a Sunday session and therefore allows more time for creative work, games, and so forth.

Simultaneously with the question of available time the question of a proper balance should be considered. Perhaps you have on your list of available materials several songs. While songs are most enjoyable and helpful, it is not wise to overbalance a program with songs. If this is done the children will tire of them, and something else that is good will have to be excluded. Decide on the number of songs and choose the very best for your purpose. Perhaps it will be only one. It is quite possible to use effectively one song only, by repeating it at intervals in the procedure.

The same discrimination should be used regarding stories. One new story should be the general rule. There should, of course, be provision for the recalling of the old ones.

We often have to make a choice between dramatization and other creative work.

It is well to remember in our planning that not all of the activities chosen should be of the very stimulating type. If you plan to use a story that requires several minutes of quiet listening, then perhaps you will plan to let the children stand by the piano as they sing, thus giving them a change of posture. If you plan for a spirited dramatization, you may plan to follow this by a rest time, in which for a few moments they will in imagination go quietly to sleep while a soft lullaby is sung to them.

Returning to our illustration of an informal procedure, and keeping the previous steps in mind, let us select the activities which will best accomplish our chosen purpose.

Songs—"Friends"[1] and "A Happy Day."[2] Both songs suggest ways of being friendly and should be used many times throughout the session.

Bible Verse—"Forget not to show love."—Hebrews 13:2a, A.S.V. (Change the words around to say, "Do not forget to show love," so that the children can make them their own more readily.)

Story—David and Jonathan—I Samuel 18:1-4.

Pictures—David and Jonathan and pictures of children at play which illustrate different ways of playing happily together.

Activities—Looking at pictures. Conversation about being friendly. (This must be timed to allow for the other activities.) Pantomiming play experiences. Actual play experiences—inviting some of the older Nursery children to be guests. (This last activity should take up at least a third of the time.)

Worship—Prayer of thanks for friends and times of play—also asking for help to remember to be friendly.

---

[1] From *Worship and Conduct Songs.*
[2] From *Our Happy World*, by Freivogel.

A Sunday Morning Session in Detail

Following are plans given in detail for a Sunday morning session, based upon the illustration used with the three steps in planning informal procedure. These plans are not to be followed to the letter, but are given as an example in which informal procedure may be used.

FRIENDS SHOW LOVE FOR EACH OTHER

Purpose

To help the children grow in their understanding of how to be friendly and in their desire to be friendly; and to provide opportunities for them to show love and consideration for others as God wants them to do.

Suggested Procedure

Looking at Pictures

When the children arrive and have placed their offering in the money basket and have taken off their wraps, a leader will guide them in finding a number of pictures placed on the tables and on the picture rail—pictures of children engaged in play activities. Each assistant should feel responsible for mingling with the groups and through tactful questions helping in the interpretation of the pictures.

Quiet Music

This will call the children together and they may be seated in a semicircle facing the leading teacher.

Conversation

The children may be led to tell of some happy times they have had during the week. During this conversation they may sing "Friends."

Song

> Friends! Friends! Friends!
> I have some friends I love!
> I love my friend and he loves me,
> I help my friend and he helps me;
> Friends! Friends! Friends!
> I have some friends I love!
>
> Friends! Friends! Friends!
> I have some friends I love!
> I share my games and share my toys

With all my friends, both girls and boys;
Friends! Friends! Friends!
I have some friends I love! [3]

Dedicating the Offering

A child may be asked to stand by the teacher and hold the basket of money while the teacher helps the children to think of how the money will be used. A simple offering song might be sung, followed by a short prayer voiced in words the children might use, such as: "Dear God, we are glad we can bring our money to our church school to help buy some of the things we have here. And we are glad that our money helps other people to know about You, too. Amen."

The basket of money may then be given to the secretary or one of the assistants.

Skipping Activity and Song

The teacher may suggest:
"We all like to come to church school where we are friends, and we like to do things together. Let's all take hands and skip around as we sing about friends again."

Story

After the children are seated, the teacher may tell the story of David and Jonathan, holding the Bible in her lap as she does so.

DAVID AND JONATHAN

I Samuel 18:1-4

David had been very brave in a battle and the king had asked him to come to the palace so that he might thank him. There at the palace he met Jonathan, the king's son. Just as soon as Jonathan saw David, he said to himself, "I surely would like to have David for my friend." And when David saw Jonathan, he said to himself, "I surely would like to have Jonathan for my friend." So they were friends and they loved each other very much.

They talked with each other and had long walks, and perhaps they went hunting together, for both of them knew how to shoot bows and arrows.

Because they loved each other so much, they wanted to do something for each other. Now Jonathan was the king's son and had almost anything he wanted. So he took his nice coat and gave it to David. Then he gave him his bows and arrows and his sword. David was just a shepherd boy who looked after his father's sheep. He had no such presents to give Jonathan. But he could help him and love

---

[3] From *Worship and Conduct Songs.* Copyright 1924, by Elizabeth McE. Shields.

him, and that is just what he did. And so Jonathan and David loved each other for as long as they lived.

Using Picture and Bible Verse

A large picture of the story may be shown as the teacher helps the children think of how Jonathan showed his love for David by sharing his things with him.

With the Bible open to Hebrews 13:2a, she may say, "God wants us to show love to friends and to people we do not know well. He says in the Bible, "Do not forget to show love." (The American Standard Version—"Forget not to show love"—is more understandable to children than the other versions, but even that sounds stilted to young children. If the words are moved around to say, "Do not forget to show love," the verse can be more readily understood and used by the boys and girls.)

Conversation, Using Bible Verse

The teacher may continue, "But how can we show other boys and girls that we love them?" Try to help the children think of definite ways, such as sharing, helping, being kind, taking turns, and other similar ways. During this conversation the Bible verse should be used several times. For instance, if a child suggests "helping someone," the teacher may say, "Yes, when we help people we are doing what the Bible says, "Do not forget to show love.""

Introducing a New Song

During this conversation a new song, "A Happy Day," may be introduced and used several times. As the children talk about taking turns and sharing, the teacher may sing the song without the piano and without any preliminary introduction.

A HAPPY DAY

When we work and play together
In a kind and friendly way,
Taking turns and sharing playthings,
We will have a happy day.[4]

After using it this way two or three times during the conversation, she may suggest that the children sing it with her as the pianist plays it. The conversation can be led around to the fact that everyone is happier and has a better time when all are kind and friendly, and then the song can be sung again. (Repetition motivated in this way is much better than any attempt at drilling.)

---

[4] From *Our Happy World* by Esther Frievogel. Copyright by Eden Publishing House, St. Louis, Mo.

Pantomiming Activity

If the children seem tired from sitting and thinking, perhaps some play experiences may be pantomimed. For instance, they may "play like" they are pushing others in swings, or climbing up a slide and sliding down, or throwing and catching balls.

Planning for Guests

In order that the children may have real play experiences, four or five of the older Nursery children may be invited to come into the Kindergarten at this time. (Arrangements with the Nursery teacher should have been made in advance, and play materials, such as dolls, doll bed, table and dishes, blocks, toy animals, trucks, and picture books, should be available.)

The teacher may say, "Would you like to invite some other children to come into our room to play with us? When they come, we must not forget to show our love. What are some of the ways we can show our love to them? . . . Yes, share our toys and be kind and help. I would like to talk to God to ask Him to help us remember to do this."

Prayer

Such a prayer may be voiced by the teacher.

Using Pictures and Song

While some child, accompanied by an adult, has gone to invite the Nursery children, the others may enjoy looking at the pictures of play experiences which were used at the beginning of the session. Different ones may choose pictures to hold and may tell the others the ways the children in the pictures are showing love. The song, "A Happy Day," may be used during this time.

Playing Together

When the guests come in, they and the children may choose desired activities. The leader and assistants should mingle freely with the different groups. They may find it advisable occasionally to sing softly, as a reminder, "I share my games and share my toys," or repeat the Bible verse, "Do not forget to show love." Ample time should be given to these play experiences.

Song and Prayer

As the time draws near for the church school to be over, the children may be called together with the music of "Friends" and all sing it. Then the leader may comment on the good time all have had, and if the children seem to be in the mood for it, she may say, "I would like to talk to God about it." Bowing her head, she may voice a prayer, such as, "Thank you, God, for the good time we have had with our friends. Help us to remember to show love to them in all our play. Amen."

Dismissal, Song

The guests may be escorted back to the Nursery while the Kindergarten children put on their wraps, and if there is time, they may sing "A Happy Day" before leaving.

Problems in Procedure

From Formality to Informality

It is not always easy to take a group of children accustomed to a formal teaching procedure and launch a procedure that is altogether informal. This is especially true of a group that is large. The effect, at times, seems to be a sort of intoxication of freedom—an aimless, disconcerting activity on the part of the children that causes an inexperienced teacher to question the wisdom of the adherents of informal teaching.

There is a happy medium between autocracy and license that should be our goal, but a wise teacher will sense the fact that some groups interpret liberty as license and she will act accordingly. For example, a teacher who had been accustomed to leading children informally took charge of a group that was not accustomed to her method. When she asked, "Can anyone find a picture that makes you think of the nighttime?" there was a bedlam of voices and a rush for the picture. Naturally, this should not be; so the next time, keeping a firmer hold with her guiding hand, she said, "I do not want you to say a word, but I want you to look very carefully at all the pictures you can see. When you find the one I am thinking of, you may put your hand on your head. I am thinking of a picture that says, 'The time of the singing of birds is come.'"

It was not long, of course, until the children learned to take turns in conversation and in the various other informal activities, but they learned gradually, and as they learned they were given more freedom.

Individual and Group Directions

Some of the problems in co-operation are easily understood if we pause to remember that the four-year-old children have been accustomed to being treated as individuals. Mother looks Frances in the eye and says, "Sit in this chair, dear," and Frances is not confused. She knows that the directions are meant for her. But when she goes to the church school Kindergarten there are perhaps a dozen other boys and girls, and the teacher says, "Let's go to the corner of the room and play we are coming to church." Frances is confused, because the directions are given to the group of children, and she has not yet learned that directions given to the group are the same as individual directions. She may be glad to enter into the activities but she does not understand that she is invited until called by name and given an individual invitation to look at the pictures, or go out into the yard, or stand by the piano.

Sometimes where it seems especially difficult for a group to follow directions, it may be well to take a moment or two, occasionally, for the use of a few very simple rhythmic games or activities where the children all do things together. In this way the children will learn to listen. A few suggestions are given in Chapter X.

A teacher should watch these little individualists and give the group directions very clearly and simply, and gradually they will learn to think "we" instead of "I."

When Visitors Come

Visitors often come to the Kindergarten, and if they are sympathetic and understanding they will not be a problem, provided there is space in the room for them. They will not comment on the responses of the children nor will they converse among themselves. The children will accept the right type and will include them in their activities.

A leader was glad to have a number of visitors on the day in the fall when she and her children went out into the churchyard to find beautiful things God had made. Many of the children were very young and were decidedly individualistic. They were quite willing to put a hand in that of a sympathetic adult and go on a walk of discovery, and they were the gainers that day because there were enough adults including the assistants to allow one adult to a group of two or three children.

Naturally it will not do for many visitors to come in at one time as this might be upsetting to the children. When uninvited guests, whom the teacher does not know, come, it would be quite within propriety for the person who greets them to invite them to sit in the back of the room and not take any part in the activities unless asked to do so by the teacher. This could be done tactfully and might save some embarrassing moments for the teacher and the children.

The pastor should be a welcome visitor, and should be drawn into the group and made to feel at home. In fact, definite plans should be made to bring about a visit from him if he does not happen to come.

Projects in becoming acquainted with children of other races may often include visits from children of other races who are in the community, or a visit from a sympathetic missionary who will be content to answer questions and share the part of her experiences which young children can appreciate.

There are other visitors who make definite contributions to the religious education of Kindergarten children. A wise leader will sense the need for certain contacts and will plan for them.

As most of the church school contacts of the children are with women and children, it will be well to plan for helpful contacts with men. We have mentioned the pastor. The general superintendent, also, should be a welcome and frequent visitor. "Daddies" may sometimes be invited specially. A friendly man who wandered into a Kindergarten group not long ago as a visitor was welcomed and invited to join the group as they played "Big Church." His reverent participation was helpful and stimulating to the group. If we are alert to the need of the children for more contacts with men who have a contribution to make to their development, we will use and make opportunities for including these friends in our group.

There should be, if possible, a parents' class, and an understanding that from time to time a small group of parents may attend the children's session provided there is ample space.

The Offering

While the taking of the offering has a place in each Sunday's procedure, it is not possible to say just when God's blessing shall be asked on the contributions of the children. It is well for them to deposit their gifts on their arrival, because hands need to be free for the various activities of the day.

The offering basket containing the money may be brought forward at a time when it can be suitably dedicated. In an informal procedure it is not always possible to specify the time in advance; in fact, it is not always possible to find a suitable time during the actual session with the children. But no harm would be done if, once in a while, the dedication was omitted, so long as the children really understand why they bring their money and how it is used.

Suggestions for the offering dedication are found in Chapter X.

Observance of Special Days

It is occasionally a problem to include special days in our church school program and to vitalize them in the experience of our children. Of course there is no question of the value of Thanksgiving and Christmas and Easter. They can and should be meaningful. Most teachers' helps not only recognize them, but build their procedure for several weeks around the experiences which culminate in these special days. The problem, as a rule, is to fit the Kindergarten plans into the plans of the whole school. Sometimes, in an effort to co-operate with the adult departments, the Kindergarten leaders will let their children take part in a big program, and thus cause their children to lose the real meaning of the day that should stand out in a special way. On the other hand, general superintendents and church school officers are quite reasonable when reasons are clearly given why these youngsters should not take part in the general school programs. There are, of course, exceptions, but as a rule the observance of Thanksgiving or Christmas or Easter is most meaningful when it takes place in the Kindergarten room and is the culmination of the activities of several weeks. Then the children will not become frightened or nervous over being "shown off" for the pleasure of adults.

Some churches feel that there are special occasions when the whole church school, including the Kindergarten children, should meet as a big family. Even at these times, it is best to let the children remain only a few minutes, make their contribution, and retire to their own room. Such occasions call for careful planning, if the children are to be safeguarded. Unless there is co-operation on the part of all the adults in the church, it is difficult to keep the children from feeling that they are "showing off." On the other hand, a Kindergarten leader with the right viewpoint can help her children to feel that they are a part of the church family and are glad to share with the rest of the family one of their songs. They need not drill or rehearse the song. They should not be exploited in any way. They may gather about the piano with their leader and not suffer the embarrassment or injury that sometimes result from "marching" to the platform and facing a sea of adult faces. If we would make the special days red-letter days to these children, we must think of the children and their pleasure rather than of the pleasure of adults only.

In most cases if we care for the everyday experiences of our children, the special days will care for themselves, because they will be a part of these experiences.

The Extended Session

By "Extended Session" we mean extra time given by the church school—time beyond the traditional hour on Sunday.

In some schools this extended session is an extension of the time of the Sunday session. The children are allowed to remain for two hours, or, under certain conditions, for two hours and a half. This allows for more play and more creative work. It allows also for a more leisurely development—providing time for the completion of interesting experiences. This type of extended session, however, requires better-trained teachers. Obviously, unless the learning experiences of the children are happy and worth while it is not well to prolong such experiences. Where a real need for this type of expansion is felt by the leaders, this need should be met; but schools should prepare carefully both from the standpoint of leadership and that of gaining the co-operation of the homes before engaging in a longer session.

One of the criticisms of extended sessions by thoughtful parents is that the children may become too tired or over-stimulated by such a long time spent in the Kindergarten room. This is true if they are overcrowded or if they are expected to remain quiet without much activity. Children must be active—it is the way they are made—and therefore it would be doing them a great injustice to expect them to sit at tables and do handwork or something similar during this extra time. But if special plans are made for a complete two-hour session in which everything will carry out the same lesson purpose; if activities are chosen which will allow the children to move about freely; and if provision is made for a simple lunch and a short rest time; then the children will not become too tired, and will benefit greatly from this longer time spent together.

For instance, in the sample informal procedure given in this chapter, if it were a two-hour session the Nursery children might be invited to come during the second hour. Then in the procedure during the first hour, the time for the conversation periods would not have to be made short, as would be necessary to allow for actual play experiences in a one-hour session. Also there would be time to allow the children to dramatize how they entertain their guests at home, using the song, "A Happy Day," during the playing of these experiences. There would also be more time for choosing and talking about the pictures that show ways of playing happily together. The whole procedure could be more leisurely and there could be more time for activities that rest and relax the children.

There are several problems connected with the extended session which should be solved before such sessions are undertaken. The first one is—who will teach at this time? Many teachers feel that one hour is all that they can give; most do not want to miss the morning church services. But we do know that an extended session which is to be of value to the children cannot be turned over to just anyone. In many churches this problem is being solved by the teachers taking turns staying, along with the parent sponsors. For instance, in a department which has six teachers, two of the teachers stay (one being appointed as leading teacher for this hour) and they are assisted by the couple who are parent sponsors for the month. (The work of parent sponsors is discussed in Chapter XII.) Of course these parent sponsors, as well as all the teachers, must attend the planning meeting where all the sessions are planned for the month, and these plans should include detailed procedures for the extended sessions as well as for the first-hour sessions. If this way is followed, the teachers will miss the morning church service one Sunday out of three. Incidentally, the sharing of the leading teacher's responsibilities by the other teachers during the extended sessions provides excellent training for these teachers.

Some churches try to double their teaching staff in the Kindergarten so that there will be enough workers to take turns carrying on the extra session while others go to church. If this is done, all the teachers attend the first hour so they will know just how far the session plans have been followed.

Another problem which arises is—what about the children who do not stay for the extended session? Allowances have to be made for the dismissal of these children. In planning the sessions the teachers must be sure that the procedures for the first hour will contain enough activities that are necessary for the guidance of those who cannot stay for the full two hours. When the children are brought at the beginning of the church school session, the parents should notify the teachers whether these boys and girls may stay or will have to leave. Then the ones who must go at the end of the first hour should be dismissed singly, if possible, while the others are engaged in playing a game or in some other activity in which they are moving about. The parents or older brothers or sisters who come for these children should be encouraged to wait quietly outside the door until the children are brought out. The teachers who leave should slip out very quietly, and if the transfer from one leader to another is made during a game or some moving activity, the children will hardly know the difference.

Many of the same things that have been said of the extension of the Sunday hour apply also to the type of expansion which makes use of an additional hour or more on a weekday. This is, in some respects, easier to handle, because the children are stimulated for a shorter time.

The whole question of an expanded session is one that needs careful study. We know that the church is not giving enough time to the religious education of its children, and this may be the solution of the problem.

For Assignment and Discussion

1. What is meant by a balanced procedure?
2. As you review the suggestions for program procedure given in this chapter, do you note any changes which you can make in your usual method of teaching which will make it more effective?
3. Select one of the following experiences of children which seems to you most fruitful for religious development. Plan in detail how you would develop it religiously.

Planting a garden.
Going to bed at night.
Going into the church auditorium.
Hearing stories of Jesus.
Making a gift for the minister.

Helpful Pamphlets

Four and Five Year Olds at School, Association for Childhood Education, Washington, D. C.

Denominational leaflets and pamphlets.

National Council leaflets and pamphlets.

Denominational and interdenominational magazines.

Denominational curricula for Sunday, weekday, and vacation sessions of the church school.

CHAPTER XII

Parents and Teachers Working Together

Both the parents and teachers of church school children are concerned with the Christian development of these children. It is essential that the church school teachers know home experiences and build on them, and essential that the parents know what is initiated and discussed in the church school that they may build on it.

For instance, Mary comes to Sunday school angry and full of resentments because she feels the new baby brother is taking all the love and attention her parents used to shower on her. A teacher who understands this can see that she gets affection and attention to help her over this difficult time, and a visit in the home with a few tactful hints dropped to the mother may solve the problem entirely.

John's mother would not have said, "Never mind, John, I'll put the milk bottles out myself," if she had known that, a few days before, the children in the church school had decided that putting out the milk bottles was a good way to help mother.

Importance of Home Training

Parents must be helped to realize that they are the *first* teachers of their children and that the home is God's first school of religion. There are many reasons why this home teaching is most important.

1. The home is a natural setting for educational procedures and has more continuity of time for them.

For example, in the church school when there are discussions about helping in the home, the children are encouraged to want to help and they dramatize ways of helping; but it is only the parents in the home who can give them the actual experiences in doing this, and it is through these experiences that they learn.

Home is the natural place for play experiences and children can be educated religiously through play as in no other way.

The best training of all is a daily religious interpretation of ordinary experiences, and this, of course, can take place only in the home. It takes time for habits of Christian ways of acting to be formed, and it is only in the home that there is time for the day by day repetition necessary for the formation of such habits.

2. There is possible in the home a better understanding of inherited tendencies and individual characteristics.

No two children are exactly alike. The church school teacher makes an honest effort to understand the individual characteristics of each child in her group, but she does not have the opportunities for this nor the background of knowledge possessed by the parents.

3. The love of parents for their children is coupled with a peculiar sense of responsibility to God.

This should make it possible for the parents to be solicitous and patient in training their children and keenly alert to their religious needs.

Because this home teaching is so important the church school must help the parents to realize their privileges and responsibilities in the Christian education of their children.

Ways in Which Parents and Teachers Can Co-operate

It is only as the home and the church school teachers co-operate and join hands in sharing the knowledge that each possesses and the experiences that each has, that the children can best develop in their Christian growth.

There are several ways in which this co-operation may be promoted.

1. Visits.

Most teachers know that there is no better means of learning about a child than visiting in his home. There they can establish a friendly contact with the parents and the child; they can observe home conditions; and they can grasp the relationship of the child to others in the family. They can explain to the parents what the church school is trying to do for the child, and suggest ways in which the parents might receive help, such as making use of parents' leaflets and books, study courses, and parents' meetings.

On the other hand, the parents should be encouraged to visit the church school department or class so that they may see what is going on and get a better understanding of methods and activities used.

2. Letters and Phone Calls.

A letter of welcome to the parents of a new child is sometimes sent before the teacher makes her first visit. If general information, as well as a welcome, is given in this letter it sometimes paves the way for an easier discussion when the personal call is made. Also letters may be sent at special seasons, such as Christmas and Easter, telling how these will be celebrated at the church school and stressing the spiritual significance of the holidays and how this may be emphasized in the homes.

Whenever the children are to bring things to Sunday school or do special things, brief notes should be sent home about them, as Kindergarten children are too young to remember to tell their parents or to report such things accurately.

Phone calls can often be made to establish friendly relationships, as inquiring when a child is sick, or reporting something nice the child did, or reminding the parents of something special.

3. Parents' Materials.

Most of the denominations publish a message to parents. These messages will help the parents to know what the children are thinking about at the church school and how they can co-operate with the teachers. The parents should be encouraged to read these and try to follow the suggestions contained therein. If the parents' materials are such that they are not taken home by the child, the teacher or her assistants should deliver them to the homes and help the parents see what use can be made of them.

There are many leaflets and pamphlets published by the denominational boards, welfare boards, and the National Council of the Churches of Christ which offer parents help in meeting problems that arise. These should be made available to the parents and should be brought to the parents' attention in different ways. Also there are many splendid books which would be of help to mothers and fathers and which it would be well to place in the church library.

4. Parent Sponsors.

Many churches are using parent sponsors in the different classes and departments and this plan has proved of great value in the Kindergarten. A father and mother are asked to be parent sponsors for a short time, perhaps for six months or three months, or even just one month if there is a large number of children in the department and it would be of value to interest a large number of the parents. Of course a mother can do this job, but asking the couple to serve together creates more interest in the family, and it is definitely good to have a man in the Kindergarten. These sponsors meet with the teachers of the department to help plan for the unit of work; they contact other parents, telling them of the plans and how they can help the teachers and the children; they may help with some of the calling if necessary; and they always visit in the department and may be asked to assist with the children if needed. If there are extended sessions, the parent sponsors may help with the teaching during that hour. (See Chapter XI.)

As these sponsors work in the planning for and with the children, they never fail to become more interested in the needs and welfare of the group and give real help in many ways.

Incidentally, future teachers may be found among the parent sponsors, as the leading teacher watches them in their contacts with the children and their interest in the group.

Parents' Meetings

In many Kindergartens the parents meet with the teachers once a month or at least once a quarter for study or discussion. At this time parents and teachers may interchange experiences which they have had with the children. They may talk over together the church school plans for the coming month or quarter, so that the parents will know definitely their part in helping the children toward the outcomes desired. The songs that may be used as a part of the coming experiences may be learned by the parents, with the suggestion that they be used many times with the children in natural situations. Certain stories may be emphasized also. But the greater help will probably come from a discussion of the practice in living which can best take place in the home.

Each church—in fact, each group—must make its own arrangement as to time. If possible, arrange the time to suit both father and mother, probably in the evenings. This means that in many cases some provision must be made for caring for the children. There are some churches where the older girls will be glad to render this service "gratis" as a class or individual activity.

There is always the possibility of afternoon meetings, but this usually eliminates the attendance of the fathers. However, meetings of the mothers are certainly well worth while and should be promoted by all means, if the other is not possible. Some churches have a meeting for fathers and mothers together once a year at night and the other meetings are for mothers in the afternoons.

One way to secure a good attendance at the afternoon

meetings is to invite the children to a party at the same time. This can be held in the Kindergarten room under the supervision of one of the assistant teachers with the help of some of the high school girls. At the same time the leading teacher and any other assistants meet with the mothers in another room.

In many situations more mothers can come to such a meeting if provision is made to care for their younger children in the nursery. Often the Nursery teacher is willing to co-operate in this way, and sometimes the Primary teacher will plan some extra activities for the older brothers and sisters in her room if the mothers cannot find someone with whom to leave them.

Of course there is always the possibility of having departmental parents' meetings after a family night supper. While the children are having a guided experience in a separate room, the parents may meet with the teachers of the various groups.

All meetings for parents must be made interesting and worth while or the parents cannot be expected to attend. They should be kept within a set time limit and there should be some time allowed for fellowship. Often the parents are asked to list topics they would like discussed at such meetings.

A Typical Program for a Parents' Meeting

Topic—A better understanding of the prayer life of a little child.

Music

Discussion: Kindergarten plans for the units of the month or quarter, including purposes, special activities, and how parents can help the children toward the desired goals.

Songs which will be used with the children during the month or quarter.

Announcement of topic for discussion.

Short devotional on prayer.

Discussion: Values and Dangers of Form Prayers, led by a parent.

Discussion: Informal Prayers. Several parents should contribute to this discussion, telling of the spontaneous informal prayers of their children and their method of leading the children into a natural communion with God.

Review of booklet, "Teaching a Little Child to Pray," by Milton.

This should be reviewed by a parent or one of the teachers and afterward circulated.

Closing prayer.

Time for fellowship.

Parent Study Groups

In some churches it is possible to form short-term parents' classes that meet on Sunday while the children are in the church school. These classes spend a large part of their time in studying the religious education of children. Sometimes a study book is selected, and sometimes topics for study are selected and assigned for discussion ahead of time. One quarter of the regular Sunday school year may be used for this study. This will mean that for three months in the year young fathers and mothers will omit the regular Bible class lesson, which they are studying for their own enrichment, and will study the religious education of their children.

Many churches have two classrooms available—one for the men's Bible class and one for the women's Bible class. Perhaps it would be possible for three months in the year to combine the men and women into two classes—and have a "Men's and Women's Bible Class," and a "Parents' Class." This would provide a room for the parents' class and would allow for choice, so that none need be forced to enroll.

The best available leader in the community should be chosen for this class.

Blessed are the children whose parents and teachers study together and plan together and work together so that these children may rightly grow in the nurture and admonition of the Lord.

For Assignment and Discussion

1. Map out a practical plan by which your own church may help to train the parents of its children.

2. Plan a series of four Kindergarten parents' meetings for the year, choosing the general topics and telling why you chose those topics.

3. Plan in detail a program for a parents' discussion group, developing one of the following topics:

How Religion Is Taught in the Home.
Home Discipline.
How Children Learn to Know God.

Helpful Books and Pamphlets

Our Little Child Faces Life, Odell
Our Family Grows Toward God, Odell
Opening Doors of Childhood, Sherrill
Parents and Children Go to School, Baruch
Their Rightful Heritage, Taylor
Teaching Religion in the Home, McAfee and Brown
Home and Church Work Together, National Council of Churches of Christ
Denominational leaflets and pamphlets
Pamphlets of the Public Affairs Committee
Booklets of the Parent-Teacher Series, Teachers' College, Columbia University